sew a
backyard adventure

21 Projects—Teepees, Hats, Backpacks, Quilts, Sleeping Bags & More

Everything you need for camping out or camping in

Susan Maw and Sally Bell of Maw-Bell Designs

C&T PUBLISHING

Text copyright © 2013 by Susan Maw and Sally Bell

Photography and Artwork copyright © 2013 by C&T Publishing, Inc.

Publisher: Amy Marson

Creative Director: Gailen Runge

Art Director: Kristy Zacharias

Editors: Lynn Koolish and Jill Mordick

Technical Editors: Susan Nelsen and Alison Schmidt

Cover Designer: Kristen Yenche

Book Designer: Christina Jarumay Fox

Production Coordinator: Zinnia Heinzmann

Production Editor: Alice Mace Nakanishi

Illustrators: Susan Maw and Sally Bell

Photo Assistant: Mary Peyton Peppo

Style Photography by Jesse Maw and Wyatt Maw, unless otherwise noted; Flat Quilt Photography by Christina Carty-Francis and Diane Pedersen of C&T Publishing, Inc., unless otherwise noted

Published by C&T Publishing, Inc., P.O. Box 1456, Lafayette, CA 94549

Library of Congress Cataloging-in-Publication Data

Maw, Susan (Susan Lou)

Sew a backyard adventure : 21 projects; teepees, hats, backpacks, quilts, sleeping bags & more / Susan Maw and Sally Bell of Maw-Bell Designs.

pages cm

ISBN 978-1-60705-667-6 (soft cover)

1. Machine sewing. 2. Camping--Equipment and supplies. 3. Children's paraphernalia. I. Bell, Sally (Sally Lee) II. Title.

TT715.M375 2013

646.2--dc23

2012049278

Printed in Korea

10 9 8 7 6 5 4 3 2 1

ACKNOWLEDGMENTS

Thanks to ...

The team at C&T Publishing for help and support to bring our vision to life

Prym Consumer USA Inc. for generously providing us with notions and tools

Jesse and Wyatt Maw for all the location photography

Nancy Janikowsky, Marie Lanier, Jennine Jones, and Nickolette Neff for their contributions to our designs with their beautiful sewing, quilting, and binding

All our willing little campy kid models—Brooklyn, Tristen, Cadence, Payton, Raimey, Mason, Joseph, and Emory, and their very patient moms, Nickolette, Haily, Anita, Stacy, Jenny, and Julianne

Our husbands, Steve and Danny, for not complaining too loudly about the fabric, batting, quilts, patterns, and everything else that we scatter about

DEDICATION

We would like to dedicate this book to mothers and grandmothers everywhere who devote special time getting to know their children by playing, creating, singing, and cooking—whether it be over a backyard grill or on the hiking trail. We all have so much to learn from each other, and there is nothing more insightful than what comes from a child's mind. In writing this book, we are encouraging all of us to get outdoors, to learn from each other, and to teach our little ones about nature and loving each other. We feel fortunate that our mother and grandmother did just that.

contents

little explorer

Campy Kids Vest

Little Explorer
Cargo Shorts

Sunshine Off
My Shoulders Hat

Campy Dog Gear

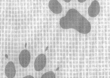

gus prints

Explore Dream Discover
—MARK TWAIN

campy kids vest

Designed and made by Susan Maw

CHILD SIZES: *Small (3–4), medium (5–6), and large (7–8)*

Campy kids can pack lots of things in our easy-on, easy-off vest with plenty of pockets. Make this classic fishing vest in a fun, colorful fabric to suit the occasion, such as camping, fishing, or attending a sports activity.

MATERIALS

Suggested fabrics: Cotton, lightweight denim, twill, and corduroy

	SMALL	MEDIUM	LARGE
Upper vest	½ yard	½ yard	½ yard
Lower vest	½ yard	½ yard	½ yard
Vest lining	½ yard	⅝ yard	⅝ yard
Extra-wide double-fold bias tape	1 package	1 package	1 package
½"-wide hook-and-loop tape	1"	1"	1"
¾" D-rings	2	2	2
7" zippers—all coordinating lower vest fabric	3	3	3

CUTTING

Locate the Campy Kids Vest pattern pieces A–N on pattern pullout pages P1–P3. Note that the patterns are printed on both sides of the pullout, so refer to General Sewing Instructions (page 108) to prepare tissue paper patterns. Cutting instructions are on each pattern piece. Label each cut pattern piece with the pattern letter and transfer any pattern markings.

Vest pattern pieces:

- **A:** Upper Vest Front
- **B:** Lower Vest Front
- **C:** Pocket
- **D:** Upper Pocket Side Panel
- **E:** Flap Tab
- **F:** Upper Pocket Flap
- **G:** Zipper Pocket Side Panel
- **H:** Lower Pocket Side Panel
- **I:** Outer Pocket
- **J:** Lower Pocket
- **K:** Tab
- **L:** Back Pocket
- **M:** Lower Back
- **N:** Upper Back

SEWING

A ⅝" seam allowance is included in the pattern pieces unless otherwise noted.

Upper Front Vest Pockets

1. Using the outside fabric pieces, stitch an Upper Front A to a Lower Front B, matching notches. Press the seams toward the lower front. Edgestitch (page 108) along the seams of the lower sections and then topstitch (page 109) ¼" from the seam edges as shown. Repeat for second side.

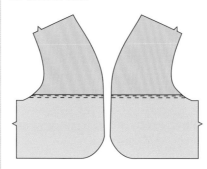

2. To make an inverted pleat in an Upper Pocket C, bring together the dotted lines, right sides together, matching small and large dots. Stitch on the dotted line to the dots from each raw edge as shown. Baste between the small and large dots. Repeat on the second pocket.

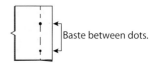

Baste between dots.

3. Press the pleat flat, centering over the seamline. Baste across the upper and lower edges of the pleat on each pocket. Remove the basting between the small and large dots.

4. To reinforce each Upper Pocket Side Panel D, stitch along the seamline for 1" on each side of the large dots, stitching through the large dots. Clip to the large dots.

5. Turn the opposite long edge of each side panel to the inside along the ⅝" seamline. Press.

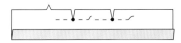

6. With right sides together, match notches and pin a side panel to each Pocket C, matching large dots on the side panels to the large dots at lower corners of the pocket, and stitch. Press the seam toward the pocket. Edgestitch the pocket sides and lower edges.

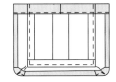

7. Press under ¼" on the upper edge of each pocket and side panel. Turn the upper edge to the inside on the fold line, forming the facing. Stitch the facing at the inner edge.

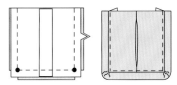

8. Pin the pocket side panel to the upper vest front, matching the upper corners of the side panel to the small dots on the upper front, and matching the small dots on the side panel to the lower corners of the pocket line. Edgestitch in place along the side panel. Repeat for the second pocket.

9. Fold the upper edge of the pocket flat, over the side panel. Reinforce the upper side edges of each pocket by stitching through all the thicknesses and over the previous edgestitching.

Reinforce stitching.

10. Press each Flap Tab E along the fold line, wrong sides together. Open out the fabric and press the raw edges to meet at the center crease. Refold, press, and then edgestitch the pressed edges. Slide the tab through the D-ring and pin the ends together. On the outside of Upper Pocket Flap F, center the tab on the right side of the fabric and baste so that the raw edges are even.

11. Place an Upper Pocket Flap F facing, right sides together, with a flap/tab unit from Step 10. Stitch on 3 sides, leaving the top edge open as shown. Trim the seam allowance and corners. Turn right side out and press. Baste the raw edges at the top together. Edgestitch the finished edges.

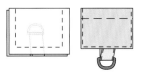

12. With the right sides together, pin a flap to each upper vest front above the Pocket C placing the ⅝" seamline on the placement lines and small dots. Stitch. Trim the flap seam allowance to a scant ¼", being careful not to cut the vest front.

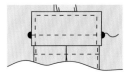

13. Turn each flap down over the seam and press. Topstitch the upper edge of the flaps, encasing the seams.

Lower Front Pockets

1. To reinforce each Zipper Pocket Side Panel G, stitch along the seamline for 1" on each side of the large dots and stitch through the large dots on one edge. Clip the seam allowance to the large dots. Press under ⅜" on the opposite edge of the zipper pocket side panel. Pin the pressed edge, right side up, to the right side of a closed zipper along the zipper teeth, extending the panel ends evenly beyond each end of the zipper tape. Stitch close to the pressed edge using a zipper foot. Repeat with the second zipper pocket side panel. Make 2.

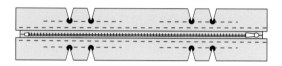

2. To reinforce both Lower Pocket Side Panel H pieces, staystitch along the seamline for 1" on each side of the dots, stitching through the dots. Clip the seam allowance to the dots. Make 2.

3. Stitch a lower pocket side panel to a zipper unit at each short end. Press the seams toward the lower pocket side panel. Make 2.

4. Turn a long edge of the side panel unit to the inside along the seamline and press. For the second side panel unit, turn the opposite long edge to the inside so that the zipper pulls are at opposite ends.

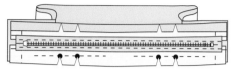

5. Press under ¼" on the straight edge of Outer Pocket I. Turn the upper edge to the inside on the fold line, forming the facing. Stitch the facing at the inner edge. Make 2.

6. With right sides up, pin the outer pocket to the Lower Pocket J, matching the sides and lower edges as shown. Baste. Stitch through both layers on the center line of the outer pocket. Make 2.

7. Pin the side panel to the pocket, matching large and small dots. Stitch, using a zipper foot. Tip: Keep the zipper open until you reach the zipper pull. Then stop stitching with the needle down, lift the foot, move the zipper pull forward or backward out of the way, and continue stitching. Repeat for second pocket.

8. On each side of the vest, pin the side panel to the lower front, matching large dots on the side panel to large dots on the lower front, and matching small dots on the side panel to small dots on the lower front. With the zipper closed, have the zipper pull toward the front edge of the vest. Edgestitch the side panel in place. Sew the zipper as in Step 7.

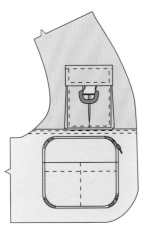

9. Refer to Upper Front Vest Pockets, Step 10, to sew Tab K (page 10). Sew the loop side of the hook-and-loop tape strip to the tab, positioning the tape 1½" from the finished end. With the raw edges even, pin the tab to the right-hand front edge of the vest, just below the seamline, with the tape facing out as shown, and baste.

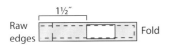

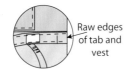

Back

1. Using a regular stitch length, stitch on the stitching line for the zipper opening on Back Pocket L. Clip through the center and into the corners. Press under these seam allowances. Pin the pressed edges, right sides up, to the right side of the closed zipper, placing the edges along the zipper teeth and centering the zipper in the opening as shown. From the right side of the fabric, stitch close to the pressed edges using a zipper foot.

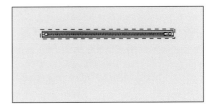

2. Press the back pocket side edges under on the seamline. Pin Pocket L to Lower Back M, matching centers, having the top and bottom edges even, and placing the side edges of the pocket on the placement lines. Baste the top edges at a ⅝" seamline and the bottom edges at a ⅜" seamline. Edgestitch the pocket sides in place.

3. Staystitch the Upper Back N neck edge ⅜" from the cut edge. Staystitching will not be shown in the following illustrations.

4. Match centers and stitch the upper back to the lower back. Press the seam toward the lower back. Edgestitch along the seams of the lower back and then topstitch ¼" from the seam edges as shown.

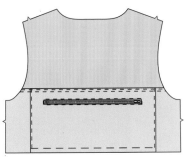

Finishing

1. Stitch the fronts to the back at the shoulder seams, matching notches. Press the seams open.

2. Stitch the fronts to the back at the side seams, matching notches. Press the seams open.

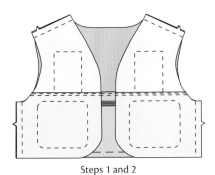

Steps 1 and 2

3. Stitch an Upper Front A of lining fabric to a Lower Front B of lining fabric, matching notches as you did in Step 1 of this project. Press the seam toward the lower front. Edgestitch and then topstitch ¼" from the edge-stitching on the lower sections.

4. Staystitch the Upper Back N lining neck edge ⅜" from the cut edge. Stitch the upper back lining to the Lower Back M lining, matching centers, similar to Back, Steps 3 and 4

(pages 12 and 13). Press the seam toward the lower back. Edgestitch and then topstitch ¼" from the edgestitching on the lower section.

5. Stitch the front lining to the back lining at the shoulder seams, matching notches. Press the seams open.

6. Stitch the front lining to the back lining at the side seams, matching notches. Press the seams open.

7. With the wrong sides together, pin the lining inside the vest, matching seams and centers, and having raw edges even. Baste the raw edges together with a ⅜" seam. Beginning at a side seam, encase the front, neck, and lower edges of the vest between the folds of the double-fold bias tape, placing the wider side on the inside and wrapping around the edge to the outside. Turn under the ends to finish. Stitch close to the edge of the bias tape on the outside, catching all layers. Tack the ends together. Finish the armhole edges with the bias tape in the same way as the vest, starting at the bottom of the armhole.

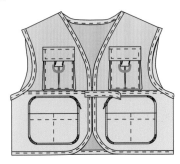

8. Sew the hook side of the hook-and-loop tape strip to left lower front just under the seamline and past the bias tape.

little explorer cargo shorts

Designed and made by Susan Maw

CHILD SIZES: *4, 5, 6, and 7*

Our cargo shorts give campy kids plenty
of pockets for stashing their stuff!

MATERIALS

Suggested fabrics: Cotton, lightweight denim, twill, and corduroy

	SIZE 4	SIZE 5	SIZE 6	SIZE 7
Shorts	1⅓ yards	1⅓ yards	1⅓ yards	1½ yards
Lightweight interfacing 20″ wide	⅛ yard	⅛ yard	⅛ yard	⅛ yard
¾″-wide elastic	½ yard	½ yard	½ yard	½ yard
⅝″ buttons for pockets	4	4	4	4
¾″ button for fly	1	1	1	1
7″ zipper	1	1	1	1
Finished length	14¼″	14¾″	15¼″	15¾″

CUTTING

Locate the Little Explorer Cargo Shorts pattern pieces A–P on pattern pullout pages P1–P3. Please note that the patterns are printed on both side of the pullout, so refer to General Sewing Instructions (page 108) to prepare tissue paper patterns and for sewing tips. Cutting instructions are on each pattern piece. Label each cut pattern piece with the pattern letter and transfer any pattern markings.

Shorts pattern pieces:

- **A:** Pocket
- **B:** Front
- **C:** Side Front
- **D:** Back Pocket
- **E:** Back
- **F:** Back Pocket Flap
- **G:** Trinket Pocket
- **H:** Cargo Pocket
- **I:** Cargo Pocket Side Panel
- **J:** Cargo Pocket Flap
- **K:** Fly
- **L:** Underlap
- **M:** Right Waistband
- **N:** Left Waistband
- **O:** Back Waistband
- **P:** Belt Loops

SEWING

A ⅝″ seam allowance is included in the pattern pieces unless otherwise noted.

Front and Back Pockets

1. For each front piece, stitch Pocket A to Front B, matching large dots. Press the seam toward the pocket.

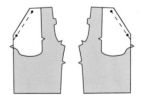

2. Turn the pockets to the inside and press. Edgestitch (page 108) and then topstitch (page 109) ¼″ away.

3. On each front section, stitch Side Front C to the pocket at the outer edge of Pocket A, keeping the front free.

4. Baste the upper and side edges of each front section.

5. To make an inverted pleat in each Back Pocket D, bring the dotted lines right sides together, matching small and large dots. Stitch on the dotted line to the dots from each raw edge as shown. Baste between the small and large dots.

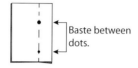

Baste between dots.

6. Press the pleat flat, centering over the stitching. Baste across the upper and lower edges. Remove the basting between the small and large dots.

7. Press under ¼" on the upper edge of the pockets. Turn the upper edge to the outside on the fold line to form the facing. Start at the fold line and stitch on the seamline around the perimeter of the pocket, on the raw edges, pivoting at the corners. Trim corners.

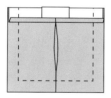

8. Turn the facing to the inside. Fold the pocket seam allowance on the line of stitching to the back and press. Stitch across each pocket at the bottom of the facing as shown.

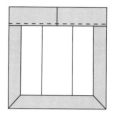

9. Pin the pockets to the shorts Back E, matching the upper corners of the pocket to the small dots on the back, and aligning the pocket with the pocket placement line. Edgestitch the sides and lower edge and then topstitch ¼" away.

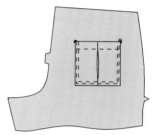

10. For each flap, with right sides together, stitch a Back Pocket Flap F to a Back Pocket Flap Facing F, leaving the top edge open as shown. Trim the seam and clip corners. Turn right side out and press. Baste the open raw edges together at the top. Edgestitch and then topstitch the finished edges ¼" from the edgestitching. On the outside of the flap, make a buttonhole at the marking. Refer to your sewing machine manual for buttonhole instructions.

11. With the right sides together, pin a flap to each back, above the pocket, placing the ⅝" seamline on the placement lines and matching the ends of the seamline to the small dots. Stitch on the seamline. Trim the flap seam allowance to a scant ¼", being careful not to cut the shorts back.

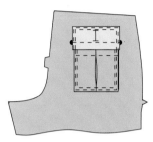

12. Turn the flap down over the seam and press. Topstitch the upper edge of the flap, encasing the seam allowance. On the pocket, mark placement of the button under the flap and sew it in place.

Cargo Pockets

1. Press under ¼" on the upper edge of Trinket Pocket G. Turn the upper edge to the outside on the fold line, forming the facing. Starting at the fold line, stitch along the seamline on the raw edges, pivoting at the corners. Trim the corners. Turn the facing to the inside. Press under the pocket seam allowance on the line of stitching. Stitch the fold at the inner edge as shown. Make only a single trinket pocket.

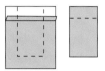

2. Pin the trinket pocket to one Cargo Pocket H, matching the upper corners of the trinket pocket to the small dots on the lower pocket and aligning with the pocket line as shown. Edgestitch the sides and lower edge. This pocket will become the right-hand cargo pocket.

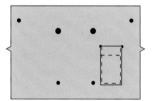

3. To make an inverted pleat in each Cargo Pocket H, refer to Steps 5 and 6 (page 16) for the back pocket.

4. To reinforce both Cargo Pocket Side Panel I pieces, stitch along the seamline for 1" on each side of the large dots, stitching through the large dots. Clip to the large dots.

5. Turn the opposite long edge of the side panel to the inside along the seamline and press.

6. Pin a side panel to each Cargo Pocket H, matching notches and placing large dots at the lower corner seamline. Stitch, pivoting at the large dots. Press the seam toward the pocket. Edgestitch and then topstitch ¼" away on the sides and lower edge through the pocket and side panel.

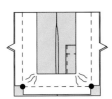 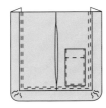

7. Press under ¼" on the upper edge of each pocket and side panel. Turn the upper edge to the inside on the fold line, forming the facing. Stitch the facing at the ¼" folded edge.

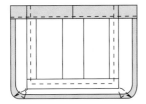

Assembly

1. Stitch the shorts front to the shorts back at the side seams. Press the seam toward the front. Edgestitch and then topstitch ¼" from the edgestitching.

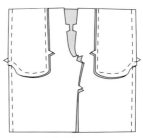

Stitch side seams.

2. Pin the cargo pockets to the shorts front/back sections, placing them over the shorts side seams, matching upper corners of the side panels to the small dots on the front and back, and matching small dots on the side panels to the lower corners of the pocket lines. Edgestitch the sides and lower edge.

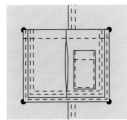

Trinket pocket is only on right-hand cargo pocket.

3. Fold the upper edge of the pocket flat, over the side panel. Reinforce the upper side edges of each pocket by stitching through all thicknesses, over the previous edge-stitching and topstitching lines. Keep Upper Pocket A free.

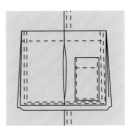

4. To make Cargo Pocket Flap J, refer to Steps 10–12 (pages 16 and 17) for the back pocket flap.

Zipper

1. Transfer the stitching line on the left front to the outside by hand basting or tracing it with chalk. To reinforce the left front, stitch along the seamline for about 1″ on each side of the large dot and through the large dot.

2. Finish the unnotched edge of Fly K. Match the large dots and stitch the fly to the shorts left front edge above the large dot. Clip the left shorts front to the reinforced large dot. Trim the seam above the clip.

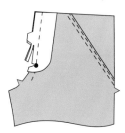

Note: It will be necessary to shorten the zipper to the measurement of the shorts opening from the large dot to the seamline at the upper edge, less ¼″. To shorten the zipper, measure down from the top of zipper the required length and make a thread bar tack. Cut off the zipper ¾″ below the bar tack.

3. Open the fly. Press the seam toward the fly. Place the closed zipper face down over the left fly with the lower end of the zipper ¼″ above the large dot and the zipper tape along the fly seam. Stitch close to the zipper on the left edge of the tape and again ¼″ away using a zipper foot.

4. Turn the fly to the inside and press.

5. Make a ⅜″ clip at the large dot in the right front. Press under ⅜″ above the clip.

6. Open the zipper. Pin the right front over the zipper tape close to the teeth, having the lower end of the zipper ¼″ above the large dot. Baste.

7. With the right sides together, fold Underlap L in half lengthwise. Stitch along the seamline on the lower edge. Trim the seam.

8. Turn the underlap right side out and press. Baste the unfinished edges together and finish the edge with a zigzag or overlock stitch, or trim with pinking shears. Pin the right front edge ⅝" over the notched edge of the underlap, having the upper edges even. Using a zipper foot, topstitch through all thicknesses over the basting.

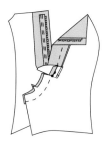

9. Stitch the fronts together at the center front seam below the zipper, matching the large dots and notches. Trim below the notches.

10. On the outside, topstitch the left front along the basting or chalk line from Step 1. Close the zipper. Bar tack through all thicknesses at the large dot and again at the end of the curve by stitching with a narrow zigzag stitch for a short distance using a close stitch length.

Waistband and Finishing

1. Stitch the backs together at the center back seam, matching the notches. Trim the seam below the notches.

2. Stitch the shorts front to the shorts back at the inner leg, matching the notches. Press the leg seams open.

3. Stitch through the center of the crotch seam a second time, just inside the seamline in the seam allowance, to strengthen this important seam.

4. Following the manufacturer's instructions, fuse the interfacing to the wrong side of Right Waistband M and Left Waistband N. Pin the right front waistband to Back Waistband O, matching the small dots. Stitch, leaving an opening between the dots and backstitching the seam at both sides of the dots. Press the seams open. Repeat with left waistband. Fold the waistband in half lengthwise, wrong sides together. Press. Unfold. Press under a ⅝" seam allowance on the edge without the dots and trim the seam to ⅜".

Unstitched openings

5. Pin the right side of the unpressed edge of the waistband to the wrong side of the shorts, matching the center backs, the seamlines of the waistband to the large dots on the shorts, and matching the notches of the waistband to the side seamline of the shorts, with the front ends extending ⅝″ over the shorts front. Stitch. Trim the seam and press it toward the waistband.

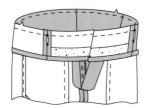

6. With the right sides together, fold the waistband in half along the fold line and stitch the front edges of the waistband. Trim the seams and corners. Turn right side out; press.

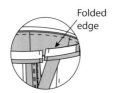

7. Turn the waistband to the outside on the fold. Pin the pressed edge of the waistband over the seam allowance. Edgestitch all edges of the waistband and then topstitch ¼″ from the edgestitching on the front and lower edges of the waistband.

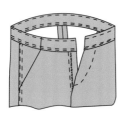

8. Make a buttonhole in the left waistband at the marking. On the right waistband, mark the button placement under the buttonhole and sew the button in place.

9. Press Belt Loops P in half lengthwise. Open, press each side in to meet the crease, and then refold. Edgestitch both long edges. Cut 5 belt loops, each 2½″ long, from the strip. Press the raw edges under ¼″. Match an end of a belt loop to the shorts at the X mark and use a narrow zigzag stitch to sew the belt loop to the shorts. Place the other end of the belt loop at the top of the waistband, aligning the belt loop, and sew in place with a narrow zigzag stitch. Repeat with the remaining belt loops.

10. Use the elastic cutting guide to cut a piece of ¾″-wide elastic. *Note:* The elastic cutting guide is approximate and may not be the proper length for your child. Measure your child's waist, multiply by 0.75, and cut the elastic that length. Use a safety pin in an end of the elastic to thread in through the first opening in the waistband and out through the other opening. Keep ½″ of each end of the elastic beyond the openings and stitch in place. Tuck the ends of the elastic under the front waistband and hand stitch the opening shut. Distribute fullness evenly.

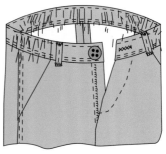

Steps 8–10

elastic cutting guide				
	SIZE 4	SIZE 5	SIZE 6	SIZE 7
Elastic	14″	15″	15½″	16″

11. Press under a 1¼″ hem allowance on the bottom edge of the shorts. Finish the raw edge or turn it under ¼″. Press. Stitch the hem in place at the inner edge and press.

sunshine off my shoulders hat

Designed by Sally Bell; made by Sally Bell and Marie Lanier

This sun hat will keep the kids cooled off and shaded
from the sun's rays while they play. We have a girl's style
with raw-edge ruffles and a boy's style with a wool bear
or fish emblem appliquéd on the front.

Hat Sizes

	SMALL (3–4)	MEDIUM (5–6)	LARGE (7–8)
Head circumference	20¼"	20¾"	21¼"

 MATERIALS

Suggested fabrics: Cotton, lightweight denim, twill, and corduroy

Yardages are the same for all sizes.

- **Hat with ruffles:** ¾ yard
- **Hat without ruffles:** ½ yard
- **Lining and bias binding:** ⅝ yard
- **Fusible interfacing 20"-wide:** ¾ yard (for example, Shape-Flex)
- **Grosgrain ribbon:** ⅝" wide, 26"
- **Cord stop:** 1

Optional:

- Wool scrap for bear or fish
- Freezer paper

CUTTING

Locate the Sunshine Off My Shoulders pattern pieces A–G on pattern pullout pages P1 and P2. Please note that the patterns are printed on both sides of the pullout, so refer to General Sewing Instructions (page 108) to prepare tissue paper patterns and for sewing tips. Cutting instructions are on each pattern piece. Label each cut pattern piece with the pattern letter and transfer any pattern markings.

Hat pattern pieces:

- **A:** Bear
- **B:** Fish
- **C:** Crown
- **D:** Top
- **E:** Brim
- **F:** Large Ruffle
- **G:** Small Ruffle

Additional cutting:

- Cut 2 rectangles 1½" × 12" for the ties from the hat fabric.
- Cut 42" of 1½"-wide bias binding, referring to Continuous Bias Binding (page 105) in General Quiltmaking Instructions.

🐾 SEWING

A ½" seam allowance is included in the pattern pieces unless otherwise noted.

Ties

1. Press the tie strips in half lengthwise. Open and press the edges in to meet the fold. Fold in half lengthwise again and press.

2. Topstitch ⅛" from edge. Make 2.

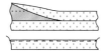

Optional: Bear or Fish Emblem

1. Refer to Wool Appliqué (page 103) in General Quiltmaking Instructions.

2. Appliqué your choice of the Bear A or Fish B in place on Hat Crown C where indicated on the pattern.

Top and Crown

1. Following the manufacturer's directions, fuse the interfacing to Hat Top D.

2. Staystitch Hat Top D a scant ½" from the cut edge. Then clip to the staystitching every 1".

3. Sew the short ends of Hat Crown C right sides together, matching the notches. Press the seam open.

4. Pin crown to top, matching the notches and matching the seam to the dot. Sew the pieces together.

5. Repeat Steps 2–4 to make the hat lining.

6. With the wrong sides together, pin the lining to the hat, matching the seams. Baste the raw edges together.

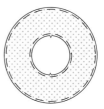

Brim

1. Following the manufacturer's directions, fuse the interfacing to Hat Brim E.

2. Baste the brim to the brim lining with the wrong sides together, ¼" from the outer edge and ¼" from the inner edge. Basting stitches will not be shown in the following illustrations.

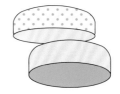

3. Staystitch the inner edge of the brim a scant ½" from the cut edge through all layers.

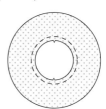

4. Referring to Curved Bias Binding (page 105) in General Quiltmaking Instructions, sew the bias binding to the outer edge of the brim, using a ¼" seam.

Optional: Brim Topstitching (Hat without Ruffles)

Topstitch the brim at 1½" and 2¼" from the inner, unfinished edge.

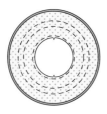

Optional: Ruffles

1. Sew the short ends of Large Ruffle F together end to end, right sides together, and matching the notches, to make a circle. Press the seams open. The outside edge of the ruffle is raw.

2. Refer to *gathering* in the Glossary of Sewing Terms (page 108). Gather the large ruffle at the top, stopping and starting again at the notches and dot.

3. Pin the large ruffle to the top of the brim, right sides up, matching the notches and the ruffle seam to the dot on the brim. Adjust the gathers evenly and baste along the inner edge of the brim.

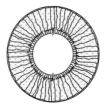

4. Repeat Steps 1 and 2 to sew and gather Small Ruffle G.

5. Pin the small ruffle to the brim on top of the large ruffle, right sides up, matching the notches and the ruffle seam to the dot on the brim. Adjust the gathers evenly and baste.

Assembly

1. Baste the ties to the bottom side of the brim at the notches, aligning the raw edges.

2. Clip the inside circle of the brim to the staystitching every 1".

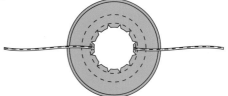

Steps 1 and 2

3. Pin the hat to the brim, matching the notches and matching the seam to the dot, right sides together. Then sew with a scant ½" seam and remove the basting.

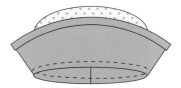

4. Cover the raw edges of the brim seam with the band edge (grosgrain ribbon) by stitching band edge as shown. Fold and lap the ribbon ends at the center back of the hat.

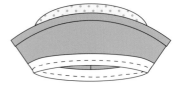

5. Turn the band and seam to the inside.

6. Thread the tie ends into the cord stop. Tie knots in the ends of the ties.

campy dog gear

Designed and made by Susan Maw

SIZE: *24" collar fits medium dogs
(about 18"–22" neck size)*

*For large dogs, increase the collar length.
For small dogs, decrease the collar length
and cut the scarf pattern smaller.*

Kids are a dog's best friend,
and now the dog can match
his kid when you make him
matching gear!

⛥ MATERIALS

- **Collar/scarf fabric:** ⅓ yard
- **Fusible interfacing:** ⅛ yard (for example, Shape-Flex)
- **Hook-and-loop tape, ¾″ wide:** 3″

⛥ CUTTING

The Campy Dog Gear template patterns A and B are on pattern pullout pages P1 and P2. Note that the patterns are printed on both sides of the pullout, so refer to General Sewing Instructions (page 108) to prepare tissue paper patterns and for sewing tips. Refer to the pattern pieces for cutting instructions. Label each piece with the template letter.

Additional cutting:

- Cut 1 piece of interfacing 1″ × 24″.

⛥ SEWING

A ½″ seam allowance is included in pattern pieces unless otherwise noted.

1. With right sides together, stitch the Scarf A pieces, leaving the long edge open. Trim the corners. Turn right side out and press. Baste the raw edges together.

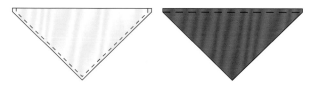

2. Press the collar strip in half lengthwise to make a center crease. Unfold the strip and position the interfacing strip along the center fold on the unmarked side of the strip, ½″ in from each end. Follow manufacturer's instructions to fuse the interfacing to the wrong side of the collar as shown. Press the seam allowance under on the interfaced edge of the collar.

3. With right sides together pin the scarf to the collar, matching centers and placing the scarf ends on the large dots as shown. Baste.

4. Press the seam toward the collar and continue to press the collar seam allowance under at each end.

5. Fold the collar over at each short end on the fold line, right sides together. Stitch the ends. Turn the ends right side out and press.

6. Fold the collar on the fold line and pin the pressed edge over the seam. Edgestitch all of the collar edges. Stitch the loop side of the hook-and-loop tape strip to the outside of the collar's left end and the hook side to the inside of the collar's right end.

Loop side of tape   Hook side of tape on back

happy trails

Happy Trails Backpack
with FUN IDEA: My Very Own ID Tag

Into the Wilds
Water Bottle Carrier

Blowin' in the Wind Quilt

white tailed deer

happy trails backpack

Designed by Sally Bell; made by Marie Lanier and Sally Bell

FINISHED BACKPACK: 8″ × 10″ × 2½″

Campy kids love to pack their stuff around—
whether it's their lunch or their new pet frog! Our
backpack is the perfect size for all kids, small and
compact with a front pocket and adjustable straps.

MATERIALS

- **Main fabric:** ½ yard for front, back, gusset, and decorative straps

- **First contrast fabric:** ⅓ yard for front trim, flap, and tabs

- **Second contrast fabric:** ⅝ yard for front pocket, connector straps, carry strap, and D-ring strap

- **Lining:** ½ yard for front, back, flap, and gusset

- **Fusible interfacing, 20″ wide:** 2 yards (for example, Shape-Flex)

- **Parachute buckles:** 3

- **1″ D-ring:** 1

CUTTING

The Happy Trails Backpack pattern pieces A–E are on pattern pullout pages P1 and P4. Note that the patterns are printed on both sides of the pullout, so refer to General Sewing Instructions (page 108) to prepare tissue paper patterns and for sewing tips. Cutting instructions are on each pattern piece. Label each cut pattern piece with the pattern letter and transfer any pattern markings.

Backpack pattern pieces:

- **A:** Back Upper Decorative Strap
- **B:** Front/Back
- **C:** Front Trim
- **D:** Flap
- **E:** Gusset

Main fabric:

- Cut 1 piece 5½″ × 7½″.

First contrast fabric:

- Cut 2 squares 3½″ × 3½″.

Second contrast fabric:

- Cut 1 piece 6¾″ × 8″.
- Cut 2 pieces 4″ × 13″.
- Cut 2 pieces 4″ × 10½″.
- Cut 3 pieces 4″ × 9½″.
- Cut 1 piece 4″ × 2½″.

Lining:

- Cut 1 piece 6¾″ × 8″.

Interfacing:

- Cut 1 piece 6¾″ × 8″.
- Cut 1 piece 5½″ × 7½″.
- Cut 2 pieces 4″ × 13″.
- Cut 2 pieces 4″ × 10½″.
- Cut 3 pieces 4″ × 9½″.
- Cut 1 piece 4″ × 2½″.
- Cut 2 pieces 3½″ × 3½″.

◢ BACKPACK CONSTRUCTION

Seams are ½" unless otherwise indicated.

Straps

Front Upper Connector Strap, Back Upper Connector Straps, Carry Strap, and D-Ring Strap

Use these pieces from the second contrast fabric: 2 pieces 4" × 13", 2 pieces 4" × 9½", and a 4" × 2½" piece.

1. Follow the manufacturer's directions to fuse the interfacing to the corresponding sizes of fabric on the wrong side of the fabric.

2. Press the pieces in half lengthwise. Open and press the edges in to meet the fold.

3. Fold in half lengthwise again and topstitch ⅛" from the long edges.

4. Label these straps:

   13" pieces = Back Upper Connector Straps

   9½" piece = Front Upper Connector Strap

   9½" piece = Carry Strap

   2½" piece = D-Ring Strap

5. Slide the female end of a parachute buckle onto an end of each of the 3 connector straps (2 straps 13" long and a strap 9" long). Fold under 3" and pin. Do not stitch yet.

Front Lower Connector Strap and Back Lower Connector Straps

Use these pieces from the second contrast fabric: 2 pieces 4" × 10½" and a piece 4" × 9½".

1. Follow the manufacturer's directions to fuse the interfacing to the corresponding sizes of fabric on the wrong side of the fabric.

2. Turn a short end under ½" and press.

3. Repeat Steps 2 and 3 of the previous section.

4. Label these straps:

   9½" piece = Front Lower Connector Strap

   10½" pieces = Back Lower Connector Straps

5. Slide the male end of a parachute buckle onto the finished end of each of the 3 straps. Fold the finished ends of the straps under 1". Stitch across the strap ½" from the end (this will keep the strap from sliding through the parachute buckle).

Front Decorative Strap

1. Follow the manufacturer's directions to fuse the corresponding interfacing piece to the 5½" × 7½" piece cut from the main fabric.

2. Press the piece in half lengthwise. Open and press the edges in to meet the fold.

3. Fold in half lengthwise again. Label this piece: Front Decorative Strap.

Back Upper Decorative Straps

1. Follow the manufacturer's directions to fuse the interfacing pieces to 2 Back Upper Decorative Strap A pieces.

2. Sew 2 Back Upper Decorative Strap A pieces (a strap with interfacing and a strap without interfacing), right sides together, leaving the short, straight end open. Trim the seams. Turn right side out and press. Topstitch the finished edges at ⅛". Make 2.

3. Match the unfinished ends of the back upper decorative strap and the back upper connector strap, centering the connector strap on top of the decorative strap, right sides up.

4. Stitch across the connector strap at 2" and 5" from the unfinished end. Repeat for the second back upper decorative strap.

5. Fold under the pinned end (with the parachute buckle) of the connector strap. Stitch it to the bottom back strap.

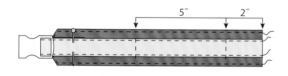

Steps 3–5

Front Pocket

1. Follow the manufacturer's directions to fuse the corresponding interfacing piece to the 6¾" × 8" piece of second contrast fabric. This is the front pocket. Also fuse interfacing to both Front/Back B pieces.

2. Sew the front pocket to the front pocket lining, right sides together, along 3 sides (2 short sides and a long side). Turn the pocket right side out and press. Topstitch ⅛" from the top finished edge (the long side).

3. With right sides up, place the topstitched edge of the pocket 3" down from the top of the backpack front, and the pocket sides 2" from the unfinished edges of the backpack front. Stitch the pocket to the backpack front ⅛" from the pocket sides. Pleat the excess pocket fabric on the lower edge of the pocket by making equal folds on each side of the center. Baste the pleats in place across the lower edge of the pocket. Press the pleats.

4. Press the long, straight edge of Front Trim C under ½". Pin the trim to the front, matching the notches on the lower edges and placing the top edge over the pocket basting stitches. Stitch ⅛" from the top edge of the trim through all thicknesses. Baste the bottom and side edges to the front.

5. Center the front lower connector strap on the front, over the pocket and front trim, matching the lower unfinished edges. Baste across the bottom edge.

6. Slide a D-ring onto the D-ring strap. Pin both unfinished ends to the backpack front, over the center front lower connector strap, matching the lower unfinished edges. Baste across the bottom edge.

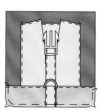

Steps 4–6

Tabs

1. Follow the manufacturer's directions to fuse the corresponding interfacing piece to the 2 pieces 3½" × 3½" of first contrast fabric. These are the tabs.

2. Fold the tabs in half diagonally, wrong sides together, to form a triangle. Press. Fold again to form a smaller triangle. Press.

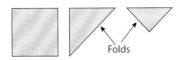

Folds

3. Insert ½" of the unfinished end of the back lower connector strap into the triangle, lining up an edge of the strap against the fold of the tab as shown.

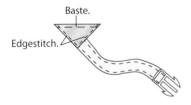

4. Topstitch 2 sides of the tab, securing the strap as you topstitch. Baste the raw edges together.

Baste.

Edgestitch.

5. Repeat Steps 3 and 4 to make a reverse strap and tab unit as shown below in Step 6.

6. Place the tabs on the backpack Back B where indicated on the pattern piece. Baste the raw edges.

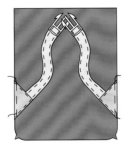

Flap

1. Follow the manufacturer's directions to fuse Gusset E with interfacing.

2. Position the front decorative strap over the center line of Flap D, matching the unfinished edges to the unfinished top and bottom flap edges. Stitch the strap to the flap, ⅛" from each long side of the strap.

3. Center the front upper connector strap on the front decorative strap, right sides up, matching the unfinished ends at the top of the flap and the buckle end at the bottom. Stitch the connector strap through all layers ⅛" from the long edges.

4. Fold under the pinned end (with the parachute buckle) of the top connector strap. Stitch it to the front decorative strap with an X as shown on the folded section.

Steps 1–4

5. Sew the flap to the flap lining, right sides together, keeping the strap free and leaving it open along the straight edge. Take care to keep the parachute buckle out of the way of the seam. Turn the flap right side out and press. Topstitch ⅛" in on the 3 finished sides. Baste the raw edges together.

◢ BACKPACK ASSEMBLY

1. Position the unfinished ends of the carry strap and the back upper connector / decorative straps to the upper unfinished edge of the back, right sides up, as shown. Pin in place.

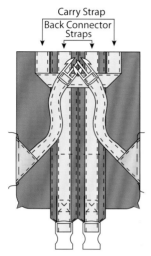

Carry Strap
Back Connector Straps

2. Center the flap on the back at the unfinished upper edge, right sides together, over the carry strap and the back upper connector / decorative straps. Baste through all thicknesses.

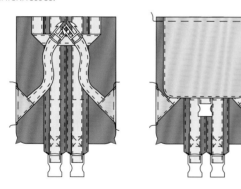

3. Sew Gusset E to the backpack front (the front has a pocket on it), right sides together, matching the notches at the bottom corners and the dots of the gusset to the dots of the backpack front.

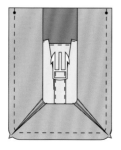

4. Repeat Step 3 to sew the gusset to the back.

5. Repeat Steps 3 and 4 with the front, back, and gusset lining pieces.

6. Place the lining inside the backpack, right sides together. Sew around the top edge, leaving a 4" opening at the front to turn. Turn right side out and press.

7. Topstitch around the top of the backpack at ⅛", folding in the seam allowance at the 4" opening and keeping the straps free.

◢ FINISHING

Slide the male ends of the parachute buckles where appropriate. Adjust as needed.

FUN IDEA!
My very own ID tag

Fun idea! Make a personalized ID tag using an embroidery machine, a sewing machine, or just a permanent marker.

into the wilds
water bottle carrier

Designed and made by Susan Maw

FINISHED CARRIER: *7" high, fits a 16-ounce water bottle*

Our water bottle carrier is insulated to keep water cool and personalized so everyone knows which water bottle is whose. It includes a detachable strap so campy kids can strap it across their chest.

◑ MATERIALS

- **Carrier fabric:** ⅓ yard
- **Lining fabric:** ¼ yard
- **Insulated batting:*** 7½″ × 10¾″
- **½″ D-ring:** 1
- **⅜″ spring snap:** 1

Optional:

- Scraps for appliqué

* We like Insul-Fleece.

Note: The instructions below call for the Deer Footprint appliqué from the *Meadow Path Quilt* project, but personalize your water bottle carrier by using any of the appliqués from *Meadow Path Quilt.*

◑ CUTTING

Locate the pattern pieces for Into the Wilds Water Bottle Carrier (pattern pullout page P1) and Meadow Path Quilt (pattern pullout page P4). Note that the patterns are printed on both sides of the pullout, so refer to General Sewing Instructions (page 108) to prepare tissue paper patterns and for sewing tips. Cutting instructions are on each pattern piece.

Carrier fabric:

- Cut 1 piece 7½″ × 10¾″.
- Cut 1 strip 2″ × 22″.
- Cut 1 strip 2″ × width of fabric.
- Cut 1 square 2″ × 2″.

Lining fabric:

- Cut 1 piece 7½″ × 10¾″.

Insulated batting:

- Cut 1 piece 7½″ × 10¾″.

◑ SEWING

A ¼″ seam allowance is included unless otherwise noted.

1. Refer to Raw-Edge Appliqué (page 103) in General Quiltmaking Instructions and *Meadow Path Quilt* appliqué block diagrams (page 66) to appliqué the desired design to the 7½″ × 10¾″ piece from the carrier fabric.

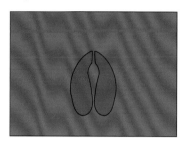

2. Mark dots on the carrier piece 1¼″ down from the top edge at a ¼″ seam allowance on both of the short edges. Baste the wrong side of the carrier piece to the 7½″ × 10¾″ piece of insulated batting.

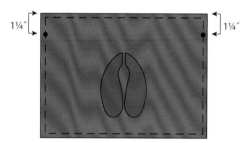

3. Press the 2″ × 2″ carrier fabric square in half, wrong sides together (this will be the D-ring tab). Open the fabric and press the raw edges to the crease. Refold and press. Edgestitch the pressed edges. Slide through the D-ring and pin the ends together. On the outside of the carrier, center the tab with the raw edges even and baste.

4. Stitch the 7½″ × 10¾″ piece of lining fabric to the carrier at the top edges with a ½″ seam allowance. Press the seam open.

5. Fold in half lengthwise, right sides together, matching the dots and the seam. Stitch the side seam, leaving a 3″ opening in the lining seam for turning the lining to the inside and another opening between the dots and the seam on the carrier to insert the drawstring later.

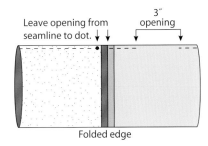

Leave opening from seamline to dot. ↓ ↓

3″ opening

Folded edge

6. Baste the wrong side of the carrier fabric Water Bottle Bottom to the batting Water Bottle Bottom. Stitch the bottom edge of the carrier to the water bottle bottom with right sides together. Tip: Sew with the carrier sides (not the circle) on top. Repeat for the lining. Turn right side out. Slipstitch the opening in the lining closed. Push the lining into the carrier.

7. Form the casing by stitching around the carrier ¾″ from the top edge. Keep the D-ring tab free.

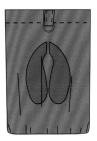

8. To make the drawstring, press the 2″ × 22″ strip in half lengthwise, wrong sides together. Open the fabric and press the raw edges to the crease. Refold and press. Edgestitch the long edges and finish the ends with a narrow zigzag stitch.

9. Pin a safety pin to an end of the drawstring and thread it through the opening in the casing. Knot the drawstring ends together. Insert a water bottle into the carrier. Pull up the strings.

10. To make the strap, repeat Step 8 using the 2″ × width of fabric strip. Slide an end through the spring snap. Overlap the ends of the strap and stitch together. Attach the spring snap to the D-ring on the carrier.

blowin' in the wind quilt

Designed and pieced by Susan Maw; quilted by Nancy Janikowsky

FINISHED BLOCK: 6″   FINISHED QUILT: 54″ × 54″

We've made this small quilt to play on, to wrap up in,
and to lie on while staring up at the sky.

MATERIALS

- **Aquas:** 1⅓ yards total of 4 different prints for blocks and borders

- **Blues:** 1⅓ yards total of 4 different prints for blocks and borders

- **Reds:** 1⅓ yards total of 4 different prints for blocks and borders

- **Greens:** 1⅓ yards total of 4 different prints for blocks and borders

- **Grays:** 1⅓ yards total of 5 different prints for blocks

- **Backing:** 3⅓ yards

- **Batting:** 60″ × 60″

- **Binding:** ¾ yard (bias cut)

CUTTING

Aquas:

- Cut 2 strips 4½″ × width of fabric.
- Cut 2 strips 2″ × width of fabric.
- Cut 4 squares 6⅞″ × 6⅞″.
- Cut 20 squares 2⅞″ × 2⅞″.
- Cut 8 squares 2½″ × 2½″.

Blues:

- Cut 2 strips 4½″ × width of fabric.
- Cut 2 strips 2″ × width of fabric.
- Cut 4 squares 6⅞″ × 6⅞″.
- Cut 22 squares 2⅞″ × 2⅞″.
- Cut 9 squares 2½″ × 2½″.

Reds:

- Cut 2 strips 4½″ × width of fabric.
- Cut 2 strips 2″ × width of fabric.
- Cut 2 squares 6⅞″ × 6⅞″.
- Cut 18 squares 2⅞″ × 2⅞″.
- Cut 8 squares 2½″ × 2½″.

Greens:

- Cut 2 strips 4½″ × width of fabric.
- Cut 2 strips 2″ × width of fabric.
- Cut 80 squares 2⅞″ × 2⅞″.

Grays:

- Cut 10 squares 6⅞″ × 6⅞″.
- Cut 4 squares 6½″ × 6½″.
- Cut 60 squares 2⅞″ × 2⅞″.

Binding:

- Cut 1 square 25″ × 25″. Refer to Continuous Bias Binding (page 105) in General Quiltmaking Instructions. You need approximately 230″ of bias strip 2¼″ wide.

⬛ BLOCK ASSEMBLY

Follow the arrows for pressing direction. Refer to General Quiltmaking Instructions (page 102).

Pinwheel Block

1. Referring to Half-Square Triangles (page 107) in General Quiltmaking Instructions, use all the aqua, green, gray, blue, and red 2⅞″ squares to piece 2″ (finished size) half-square triangle units in the following color combinations: 24 aqua/green, 16 aqua/gray, 28 blue/green, 16 blue/gray, 28 red/green, 8 red/gray, and 80 green/gray.

2. Use an aqua 2½″ square, 4 aqua/green half-square triangle units, and 4 green/gray half-square triangle units to piece an aqua Pinwheel block. Make a total of 6 blocks.

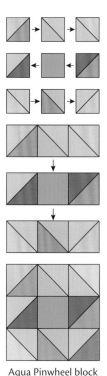

Aqua Pinwheel block

3. Use a blue 2½″ square, 4 blue/green half-square triangle units, and 4 green/gray half-square triangle units to piece a blue Pinwheel block. Make a total of 7 blocks.

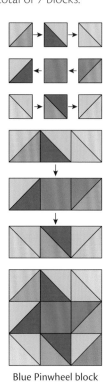

Blue Pinwheel block

4. Use a red 2½″ square, 4 red/green half-square triangle units, and 4 green/gray half-square triangle units to piece a red Pinwheel block. Make a total of 7 blocks.

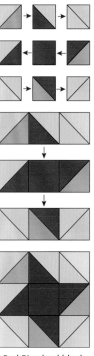

Red Pinwheel block

5. Use an aqua 2½" square and 8 aqua/gray half-square triangle units to piece an aqua/gray Pinwheel block. Make a total of 2 blocks.

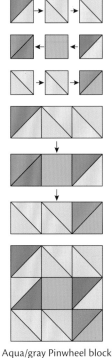

Aqua/gray Pinwheel block

6. Use a blue 2½" square and 8 blue/gray half-square triangle units to piece a blue/gray Pinwheel block. Make a total of 2 blocks.

Blue/gray Pinwheel block

7. Use a red 2½" square and 8 red/gray half-square triangle units to piece a single red/gray Pinwheel block.

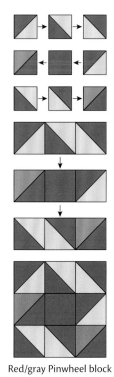

Red/gray Pinwheel block

Half-Square Triangle Block

Referring to Half-Square Triangles (page 107) in General Quiltmaking Instructions, use 10 gray, 4 aqua, 4 blue, and 2 red 6⅞" squares to piece 6" (finished size) half-square triangle units in the following color combinations: 8 aqua/gray, 8 blue/gray, and 4 red/gray.

Borders

Refer to Borders (page 103) in General Quiltmaking Instructions.

1. For the inner border, use the 2" × width of fabric strips to piece the following: a blue strip 2" × 42½", a red strip 2" × 42½", an aqua strip 2" × 45½", and a green strip 2" × 45½".

2. For the outside border, use the 4½" × width of fabric strips to piece the following: an aqua strip 4½" × 45½", a green strip 4½" × 45½", a blue strip 4½" × 53½", and a red strip 4½" × 53½".

◢ ASSEMBLY

Refer to the quilt layout diagram to assemble the quilt.

◢ QUILTING

Nancy Janikowsky machine quilted a simple allover swirl design that included the letters *A*, *B*, and *C* with the numerals *1*, *2*, and *3*.

◢ BINDING

Referring to Binding (page 104), bind the quilt with the 2¼"-wide bias strip.

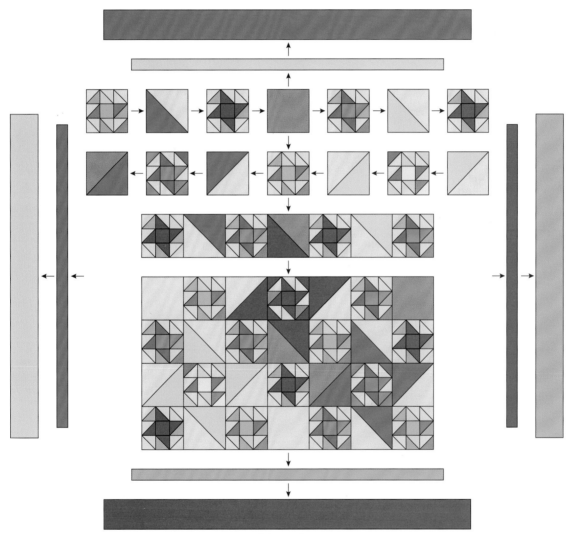

Quilt layout diagram

campy kids

red fox

happy campers teepee

Designed and made by Susan Maw

FINISHED TEEPEE: *60″ to top of teepee poles × 40″ square*

Campy kids will be happy campers when camping in
the backyard or even in their own bedroom in this
simple-to-make, kid-size teepee. We've included directions
for an optional peephole window. Parents will love the
hours of play it provides and, when it's not in use,
can just pick it up for storage.

❊ MATERIALS

- **Suggested fabrics:** Cotton, lightweight denim, and twill
  Fabric for tepee top and door pullbacks: 1 yard*
  Fabric for tepee bottom and door panels: 3¾ yards*

- **Hook-and-loop tape, ¾˝ wide:** 2˝

- **PVC pipes, ¾˝ in diameter:** 4 pipes 5´ long

- **Acrylic paint:** for ends of pipes

Optional:

- **Clear, medium-weight upholstery vinyl, 54˝ wide:**
  ¼ yard for peephole window

- **Grosgrain ribbon or twill tape to tie pipes together:**
  1 yard

* Extra fabric is needed for directional fabric design.

❊ CUTTING

Refer to General Sewing Instructions (page 108).

Teepee Bottom Panels

Refer to the cutting diagram (below) for A and C panels.

1. Square each end of the teepee bottom fabric. (We allowed an extra few inches of fabric that isn't shown on the cutting diagram.) Cut the panel 34½˝ wide × length (3¾ yards) of fabric.

2. Mark the fabric at the dots and draw cutting lines as indicated on the cutting diagram.

3. Cut 3 Teepee Bottom A pieces.

4. Cut a Door Panel C and a Door Panel C reversed. Mark the door pullback placement 8˝ down from top and 10˝ over from straight front edge, as shown in the cutting diagram.

Optional: Peephole Window

1. Make 3 circle templates: 7˝ diameter, 6˝ diameter, and 5˝ diameter.

2. Use the 7˝ template to cut a circle from the vinyl.

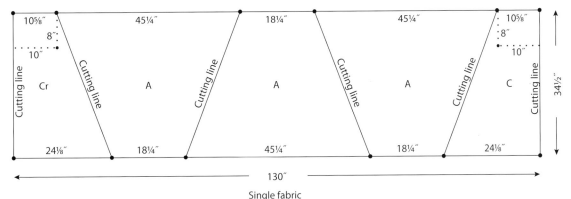

Single fabric

Cutting diagram for A and C panels

3. Refer to the diagram for the peephole placement. Find the center of the 18¼" edge of a panel A, measure down 2½", and mark. Place the top edge of the 6" template at the mark and trace around the template for the stitching line. Center the 5" template inside the 6" marked circle and trace for the cutting line.

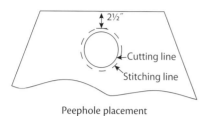

Peephole placement

Teepee Top Panels and Tie-Backs

Refer to the cutting diagram for B panels.

1. With the teepee top fabric folded double, cut a rectangle 17⅞" × 30⅝". (Because you have 2 layers, you have 2 rectangles.) Keep the pieces layered together.

2. Mark the top layer fabric at the dots and draw cutting lines as indicated on the cutting diagram. Cut through the double layers of fabric on the cutting lines to yield 4 B panels.

3. Cut 2 strips 4" × 9" from the remaining teepee top fabric.

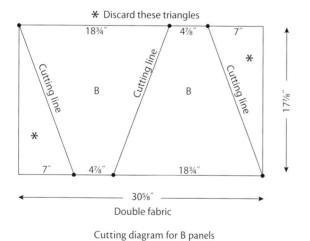

✳ Discard these triangles

18¾"   4⅞"   7"

Cutting line

B

Cutting line

B

Cutting line

✳

✳

7"   4⅞"   18¾"

17⅞"

30⅝"
Double fabric

Cutting diagram for B panels

SEWING

A ½" seam allowance is included in the pattern pieces unless otherwise noted.

1. If making the optional peephole window, stitch around the stitching line on the marked A panel. Cut out on the cutting line. Clip the seam allowance to the line of stitching and press the seam allowance to the inside. Center and pin the vinyl circle over the opening on the back side of the fabric. On the front side of the panel edgestitch and topstitch the window in place. This will be the back wall of the finished teepee. You could put a window in each section.

2. Stitch an A panel to a B panel with right sides together to make the teepee sides. Press the seam toward the bottom. Edgestitch and topstitch the seam. Repeat to make a total of 3 sides. If you made a peephole, that section becomes the back wall of the teepee.

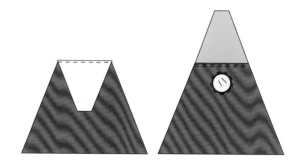

3. To narrowly hem the front edges of the door panels C and Cr, press under a ½" seam allowance along the long straight edges as shown. Open the hem and turn in the raw edges to meet the crease. Press. Refold and stitch in place. Pin the door panels to the remaining B panel, overlapping the finished edges of the door panels to fit the top as shown. Stitch. Press the seam toward the door panels. Edgestitch and topstitch the seam.

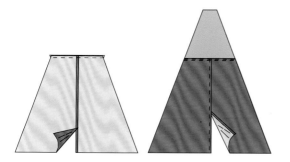

4. To make the door pullbacks, press the 2 strips 4" × 9" in half lengthwise, wrong sides together. Open the fabric and press the raw edges in to meet the crease. Turn a short end in ½" and press. Refold lengthwise and press. Edgestitch all of the edges. Cut the length of the hook-and-loop tape in half. Stitch the hook side of a hook-and-loop tape piece to the finished end of each pullback. Pin the unfinished end of the pullback to the X mark on the fabric back of each door panel, with the hook-and-loop tape facing the wrong side of the door panel. Baste. Stitch the loop side of the hook-and-loop tape piece to the exterior of each door panel at the X mark over the basting.

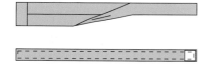

5. To narrowly hem the bottom and top edges of all 4 sides, press under a ½" seam allowance. Open out the hem and turn the raw edge in to meet the crease. Press. Refold, and stitch in place.

6. Stitch the tepee sides to the tepee back and front with a ¼" seam.

7. On the outside at the seams, press each corner seam together flat. Stitch 1¾" away from the edge of the seam to form a casing for the pipes. *Note:* Some lighter-weight fabrics should be stitched 1⅝" away from the edge of the seam. We recommend sewing about a quarter of the way down from the top on a seam and then checking the fit of the PVC pipe. You may need to adjust the width for your fabric's bulk. The casing should fit snugly, but it shouldn't be difficult to fit the PVC pipe into the casing.

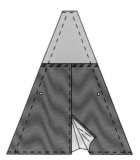

8. Edgestitch the casings closed at the bottom edge.

9. Paint the top quarter of the pipes. Allow the paint to dry. Insert the pipes into the casings.

10. Refer to the photo (page 46) to set up the teepee. Arrange the pipes at the top, adjusting them to stand with all 4 sides stretched out fully at the bottom and the pipes standing as straight as possible. (*Optional:* Tie the ribbon around the pipes at the top to help hold them together.)

li'l campers teepee

Designed and made by Sally Bell

FINISHED TEEPEE: *26″ high × 27″ square*

Samuel and Samantha Bear (page 58) need a place to hang out too. What better place than their own little teepee to match the Happy Campers Teepee (page 46)? Our Li'l Campers Teepee is just the right size for all sorts of dolls, including Barbies and GI Joes.

🐾 MATERIALS

- **Fabric:** 1⅝ yards*

- **Twine or ribbon:** ½ yard to tie dowels together

- **Wooden dowels, ¼″ diameter:** 4 dowels 29″ long

Optional:

- Acrylic paint for dowel ends

* Extra fabric is needed for directional fabric design.

🐾 CUTTING

Refer to General Sewing Instructions (page 108).

Teepee Flaps A:

Refer to the Flaps A cutting diagram.

1. With the teepee fabric folded double, cut a rectangle 14⅛″ × 21⅛″. (Because you have 2 layers, you have 2 rectangles.) Keep the pieces layered together.

2. Mark the top layer fabric at the dots and draw cutting lines as indicated on the cutting diagram. Cut on the lines through the double layers of fabric to yield 2 Flap A and 2 Flap Ar pieces.

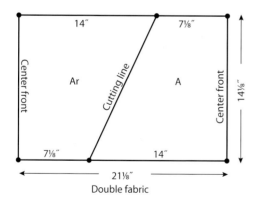

Flaps A cutting diagram

Teepee Front Top B and C Panels

Refer to Front Top B and C Panels cutting diagram.

1. Square each end of the fabric. Cut a piece 27⅞″ × 55″.

2. Working from left to right across the top and bottom edges of the fabric, mark the fabric at the dots and draw the cutting lines as indicated on the cutting diagram. Cutting on the lines yields 3 C panels and a smaller B panel.

3. Cut the pieces indicated in the diagram.

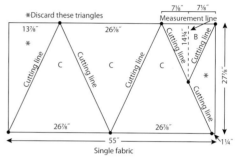

Front Top B and Teepee Back and Sides C cutting diagram

4. Refer to the diagram for the B panel to mark the dots 3″ from the tip on each side and in ½″ from the fabric edges as indicated. Mark another dot ½″ from the edge at the center of the bottom edge as shown.

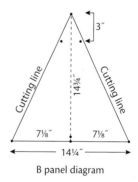

B panel diagram

5. Refer to the diagram for the C panels to mark dots 3″ down from the tips and ½″ in from the edge as you did on the B panel.

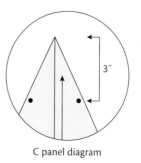

C panel diagram

🐾 TEEPEE CONSTRUCTION

A seam allowance of ½" is included on the pattern pieces unless otherwise noted.

1. Sew the 2 A panels, right sides together, down the center front and across the bottom. Turn right side out. Press. Topstitch. Baste the raw edges together. Repeat using the 2 Ar panels.

2. Sew the B panel to the A and Ar units from Step 1, matching the center edges of the front flaps to the dot on the front. Press the seam toward the front top. Topstitch the seam.

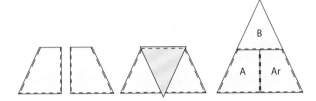

3. Make a narrow hem in the bottom edge of the 3 C panels by pressing under a ½" seam allowance. Open the fold and turn the raw edge in to meet the crease. Press and stitch in place.

4. Sew the 2 C panels, right sides together, and stop stitching at the dot 3" from the top. Add the last C panel.

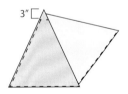

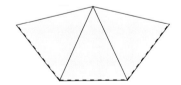

5. Sew the sides to the front section, right sides together, and stop stitching at the dot 3" from the top.

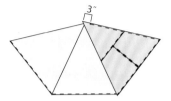

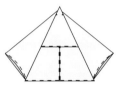

6. On the outside, press each corner seam together. Topstitch ½" from the edge of the seam to form a casing for the dowels. Stop stitching at the dot.

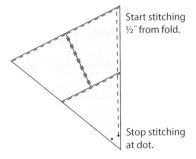

Start stitching ½" from fold.

Stop stitching at dot.

7. Edgestitch the casings closed at the bottom edge.

8. Insert the dowels into the casings. *Optional:* Before inserting the dowels, paint the top quarter of each dowel.

9. Refer to the photos to set up the teepee. Arrange the dowels at the top, adjusting them to stand with all 4 fabric side bottom edges stretched out. Tie twine or ribbon around the dowels at the top to help hold them together.

good night sleeping bag with stuff sack

Designed and made by Susan Maw

FINISHED SLEEPING BAG: *32″ × 65″*
FINISHED STUFF SACK: *11″ diameter × 23″*

No making the bed the next morning when kids sleep in their very own sleeping bag! Just roll it up and stuff it into the handy stuff sack for storage.

🐾 MATERIALS

Suggested fabrics: 45″-wide cotton, lightweight denim, and twill; flannel or brushed cotton for the lining

Sleeping bag

■ **Color 1:** ¼ yard of 4 different cotton prints for Bear Claw blocks

■ **Color 2:** ¼ yard of 4 different cotton prints for Bear Claw blocks

■ **Exterior fabric:** 3⅞ yards

■ **Lining:** 3⅞ yards

■ **High-loft batting:** 70″ × 74″

■ **Twill tape or grosgrain ribbon, ⅞″ wide:** 3 yards

■ **Hook-and-loop tape, ¾″ wide:** 12″

Stuff sack

■ **Exterior fabric:** 1⅛ yards

■ **Facing:** ¼ yard

■ **Twill tape or grosgrain ribbon, ⅞″ wide:** 1½ yards

🐾 CUTTING

Refer to General Sewing Instructions (page 108) and General Quiltmaking Instructions (page 102).

Color 1:

■ Cut 10 squares 3½″ × 3½″.

■ Cut 20 squares 1⅞″ × 1⅞″.

■ Cut 10 squares 1½″ × 1½″.

Color 2:

■ Cut 10 squares 2½″ × 2½″.

■ Cut 20 squares 1⅞″ × 1⅞″.

Sleeping bag exterior fabric:

■ Cut 1 panel 33″ × 66″.

■ Cut 1 panel 33″ × 48¼″.

■ Cut 1 panel 33″ × 12¼″.

■ Cut 8 strips 3″ × 5″.

■ Cut 2 rectangles 1¾″ × 6½″.

Lining:

■ Cut 2 panels 33″ × 66″.

■ Cut 8 strips 3″ × 5″.

Batting:

■ Cut 2 panels 37″ × 70″.

Hook-and-loop tape:

■ Cut 8 pieces 1½″ long.

Stuff sack fabric:

■ Cut 1 panel 24″ × 35½″.

■ Cut 1 circle by tracing around an 11″ dinner plate and adding ½″ seam allowance for stuff sack bottom.

Facing:

■ Cut 1 piece 6½″ × 35½″.

🐾 BEAR CLAW BLOCK

Finished block: *6″ × 6″*

All quilt blocks have a ¼″ seam allowance. Follow the arrows or written instructions for pressing direction.

1. Referring to Half-Square Triangles (page 107) in General Quiltmaking Instructions, use all the 1⅞″ squares of Color 1 and Color 2 to piece 40 half-square triangle units (1″ finished size) from Colors 1 and 2. Press the seams toward the darker color.

2. Use half-square triangle units and 2½″ squares of Color 2 to make 10 A units.

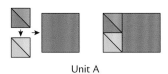

Unit A

3. Use half-square triangle units and 1½″ squares of Color 1 to make 10 B units.

Unit B

4. Use A and B units to make 10 C units.

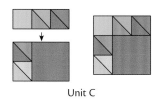

Unit C

5. Use 5 C units and 3½″ squares of Color 1 to make 5 D units.

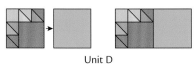

Unit D

6. Use 5 C units and 3½″ squares of Color 1 to make 5 E units.

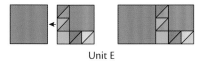

Unit E

7. Assemble the blocks by piecing D and E units to make 5 Bear Claw blocks.

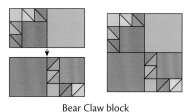

Bear Claw block

🐾 SEWING

A ½″ seam allowance is included unless otherwise noted.

Sleeping Bag

1. Sew the 5 Bear Claw blocks together in a row using a ¼″ seam. At each end of the row, sew an exterior 1¾″ × 6½″ rectangle.

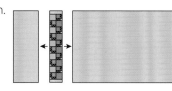

2. Stitch the block row between the exterior 33″ × 12¼″ piece and the exterior 33″ × 48¼″ piece, using a ¼″ seam.

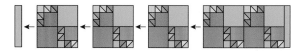

3. Mark the exterior front and back panels for quilting as shown: 3 columns lengthwise, starting with a center row, and a row 8″ out from each side of the center; 10 rows across at 6″ apart, starting 6″ from the top edge. Place marks at the intersections of the columns and rows, except where they intersect at the quilt blocks. Place the panels right side up on the batting, and pin together at the marks. Baste the panel and batting layers together at the outside edges at a ½″ seam allowance. Trim excess batting.

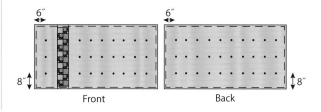

Front   Back

4. For the tabs, sew each 3" × 5" exterior piece to a 3" × 5" lining piece, leaving them open at one short end. Trim the corners. Turn right side out and press. Baste the open edges together. Edgestitch the finished edges. Sew the hook side of the hook-and-loop tape strip to the lining side of each tab, centering the strip ½" from the finished end.

5. With right sides together and the raw edges even, baste the tabs to the edge of the sleeping bag front as shown. Place the first tab ½" in from the top edge of the sleeping bag at the seam allowance. Measure down 8" from the center of the first tab to place the center of the second tab, and continue in the same 8" intervals for the remaining tabs.

6. Place the sleeping bag front, right sides together, on a 33" × 66" lining panel. Stitch the upper and left edges, catching the tabs in the seams as shown. Trim the corner and turn right side out. Baste the open edges together.

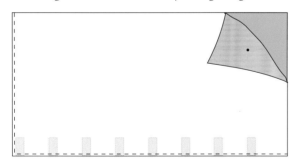

7. Quilt the layers together by machine sewing a 1" N or X shape (or a design of your choice) over each mark. Stitch across the quilt block rows at top and bottom, and between each pair of blocks.

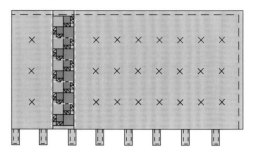

8. Mark the bottom edge of the sleeping bag front at 4" and 11" in from the side as shown. Cut the twill tape or ribbon in half. Fold each length in half and place the fold even with the raw edge of the sleeping bag at the marks. Baste.

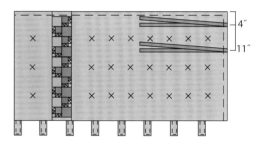

9. Baste the sleeping bag front to the sleeping bag back with right sides together at the unfinished side and bottom edges.

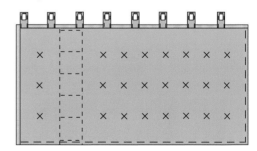

10. Press a ½" seam allowance on the bottom edge of the remaining lining panel. Sandwich the sleeping bag back, right side up, the quilted sleeping bag front wrong side / inside up, and the remaining lining panel wrong side up. Keep the finished side and top edges of the sleeping bag front free. Stitch the lining to the sleeping bag back at both side edges and the top edge. On the bottom edge, stitch over the basting, leaving the lining free. Trim corners. Turn right side out through the bottom edge. Slipstitch the pressed edge of the lining in place.

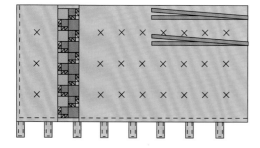

Sleeping bag back right side up
Sleeping bag front lining side up
Lining wrong side up

11. Quilt the sleeping bag back layers together, as in Step 7.

12. Topstitch ½" from the top and side edges.

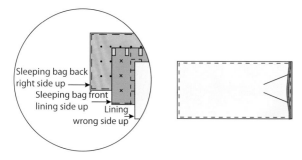

13. Sew the loop side of a hook-and-loop tape strip to the sleeping bag back through all layers, aligning them with the tabs from the front.

Stuff Sack

1. Mark the 35½" × 24" piece of stuff sack fabric, 4" and 5" down from the top edge at the ½" seam allowance on both short edges as shown.

4"
5"
4"
5"
Measure from top edge.

2. Press the 35½" × 6½" facing under ¼" to the wrong side along a long edge. Then stitch the facing to the marked piece from Step 1, as shown. Press the seam open.

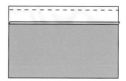

3. Bring the marked edges together, matching the seams, and stitch, leaving an opening between the marks on the stuff sack. Finish the seam with a zigzag or overlock stitch, or by trimming with pinking shears, from the bottom edge to 1" below the marks, and press the entire seam open.

4. Turn the facing to the inside and press. Stitch the facing to the stuff sack at the pressed facing edge. To form a casing, stitch 2 rows 3½" and 4½" from the top edge, using the marks as guides.

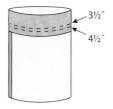

3½"
4½"

5. Sew the bottom edge of the stuff sack to the Stuff Sack Bottom. Finish the seam.

6. Pin a safety pin to an end of the twill tape or ribbon and thread it through the opening in the casing. Knot the ends. Stuff the rolled-up sleeping bag inside. Pull up the twill tape and tie closed.

samuel or samantha bear

Designed and made by Susan Maw

FINISHED BEAR: *10" high*

Kids can hug Samuel or Samantha Bear while braving that backyard camping trip!

🐾 MATERIALS

- **Suggested fabrics:** Cotton, flannel, corduroy, lightweight wool, wool blends, and fleece

- **Bear fabric:** ⅜ yard

- **Embroidery floss:** black or brown for nose and mouth

- **Buttons, ¼″ in diameter:** 2 for eyes*

- **Ribbon, ⅜″ wide:** ¾ yard

- **Polyester fiberfill**

* If the bear is for a child under three years old, stitch or paint the eyes to avoid a choking hazard from the buttons.

🐾 CUTTING

Locate the Samuel or Samantha Bear pattern pieces A and B on pattern pullout page P4. Note that the patterns are printed on both sides of the pullout, so refer to General Sewing Instructions (page 108) to prepare tissue paper patterns and for sewing tips. Cutting instructions are on each pattern piece. Label each cut pattern piece with the pattern letter and transfer any pattern markings.

🐾 SEWING

A ¼″ seam allowance is included in the pattern pieces unless otherwise noted.

1. Stitch the Bear Body Front A pieces together at the center seam. Clip the curves. Finger-press the seam open.

2. Pin the body front to the Bear Body Back B. Stitch, leaving an opening to turn. Clip the curves. Turn the bear right side out.

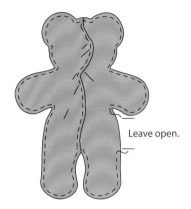

Leave open.

3. Stuff the bear firmly. Slip-stitch the opening closed.

4. Use embroidery floss to sew the nose by stitching straight stitches back and forth. Put the needle under at the nose, come up at an end of the mouth, and stitch across to the other end. Then come up in the center of the mouth and take a final stitch up to the bottom of the nose. Make a knot and hide the thread ends in the nose. Sew button eyes to the bear, taking the needle under from the first button to the second and slightly pulling to indent the bear's face at the eyes.

5. Tie the ribbon in a bow around the bear's neck.

meadow path

Meadow Path Quilt

Meadow Path Bed Skirt

Meadow Path Pillow Sham
with FUN IDEA: Trim for Sheets

Butterfly Pillow

meadow path quilt

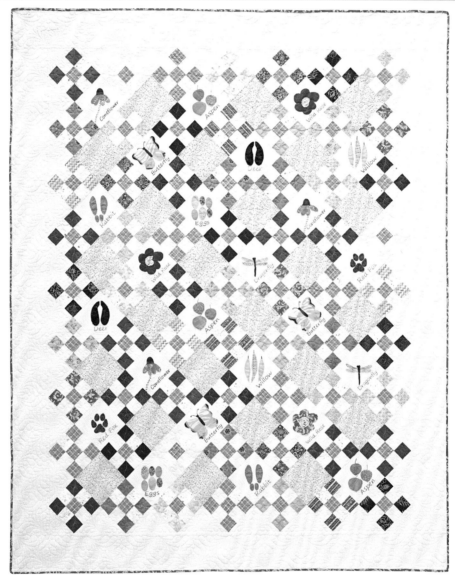

Designed and pieced by Susan Maw; quilted by Nancy Janikowsky

FINISHED BLOCK: 6″ × 6″   FINISHED QUILT: 72″ × 89″

This quilt has it all—simplicity, beauty, and nature. We have combined simple Nine-Patch blocks with nature-inspired appliqués that are beautiful. Make the entire Meadow Path bedroom set for a one-of-a-kind look.

MATERIALS

■ **Cream tone-on-tone:** 4 yards for the Nine-Patch blocks, appliqué blocks, setting triangles, and borders

■ **Cream:** ½ yard each of 2 different fabrics for the Nine-Patch blocks

■ **Peach:** 1 yard for the plain blocks

■ **Orange plaid:** ⅜ yard for center square in the Nine-Patch blocks

■ **Oranges:** ⅛ yard each of 7 different fabrics for the Nine-Patch blocks

■ **Pinks:** ⅛ yard each of 7 different fabrics for the Nine-Patch blocks, plus 1 square 7½" × 7½" from 3 pale pinks

■ **Aquas:** ⅛ yard each of 3 different fabrics for the Nine-Patch blocks

■ **Reds:** ⅛ yard each of 2 different fabrics for the Nine-Patch blocks

■ **Plums:** ⅛ yard each of 2 different fabrics for the Nine-Patch blocks

■ **Assorted scraps** of brown, green, purple, yellow, pink, and aqua for appliqués

■ **Binding:** ⅞ yard

■ **Backing:** 5½ yards

■ **Batting:** 79" × 96"

■ **Embroidery floss** in browns and greens

CUTTING

Locate the Meadow Path Quilt appliqué template patterns on pattern pullout page P4. Note that the patterns are printed on both sides of the pullout. To preserve the original pullouts, trace the patterns to make your own templates. Cutting instructions are on each piece. Label each cut pattern piece with the name.

Cream tone-on-tone:

- Cut 2 strips 6½" × 77" from the length of fabric.

- Cut 2 strips 6½" × 72" from the length of fabric.

- Cut 4 strips 6½" × width of fabric; subcut into 24 squares 6½" × 6½".

- Cut 4 strips 2½" × width of fabric.

- Cut 7 squares 11½" × 11½"; cut in half on the diagonal twice for a total of 28 setting triangles.

- Cut 2 squares 6" × 6"; cut in half on the diagonal once for a total of 4 corner triangles.

- Cut 7 strips 2½" × 16".

Creams:

- Cut 2 strips 2½" × width of fabric from each of the 2 fabrics.

- Cut 7 strips 2½" × 16" from each of the 2 fabrics.

Peach:

- Cut 4 strips 6½" × width of fabric; subcut into 24 squares 6½" × 6½" for the plain blocks.

Orange plaid:

- Cut 4 strips 2½" × width of fabric for the center square in the Nine-Patch blocks.

Oranges:

- Cut 2 strips 2½" × 16" from each of the 7 fabrics.

Pinks:

- Cut 2 strips 2½" × 16" from each of the 7 fabrics.

- Cut 3 bias strips ½" × 9" from each pale pink 7½" square.

Aquas:

- Cut 2 strips 2½" × 16" from each of the 3 fabrics.

Reds:

- Cut 2 strips 2½" × 16" from each of the 2 fabrics.

Plums:

- Cut 2 strips 2½" × 16" from each of the 2 fabrics.

Binding:

- Cut 1 square 28" × 28". Refer to Continuous Bias Binding (page 105). You need approximately 330" of bias strip 2¼" wide.

◤ BLOCK ASSEMBLY

Follow the arrows for pressing direction. Refer to General Quiltmaking Instructions (page 102).

Nine-Patch Block

1. Sew a cream tone-on-tone 2½" × width of fabric strip and a cream 2½" × width of fabric strip to an orange plaid 2½"-wide strip lengthwise to make a strip set A. Repeat to make a total of 4 strip sets.

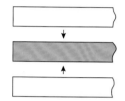

2. Crosscut the A strip sets into 63 sections, 2½" wide.

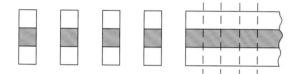

3. Sew 2 orange 2½" × 16" strips to a cream or cream tone-on-tone 2½" × 16" strip lengthwise to make a strip set B. Repeat to make a total of 7 strip sets. Crosscut the strip sets into 42 sections 2½" wide.

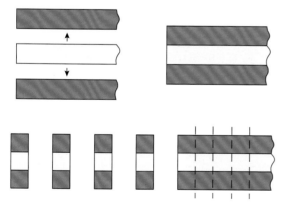

4. Sew 2 pink 2½" × 16" strips to a cream or cream tone-on-tone 2½" × 16" strip lengthwise to make a strip set B. Repeat to make a total of 7 strip sets. Crosscut the strip sets into 42 sections 2½" wide.

5. Sew 2 aqua 2½" × 16" strips to a cream or cream tone-on-tone 2½" × 16" strip lengthwise to make a strip set B. Repeat to make a total of 3 strip sets. Crosscut the strip sets into 18 sections 2½" wide.

6. Sew 2 red 2½" × 16" strips to a cream or cream tone-on-tone 2½" × 16" strip lengthwise to make a strip set B. Repeat to make a total of 2 strip sets. Crosscut the strip sets into 12 sections 2½" wide.

7. Sew 2 plum 2½" × 16" strips to a cream or cream tone-on-tone 2½" × 16" strip lengthwise to make a strip set B. Repeat to make a total of 2 strip sets. Crosscut the strip sets into 12 sections 2½" wide.

8. Refer to the Nine-Patch block piecing diagram to sew an A section and 2 B sections together. Repeat to make a total of 21 orange, 21 pink, 9 aqua, 6 red, and 6 plum Nine-Patch blocks.

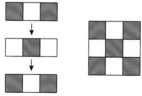

Nine-Patch block piecing diagram

Appliqué Blocks

Refer to Raw-Edge Appliqué (page 103) and Embroidery Stitches (page 109) as needed.

Use the cream tone-on-tone 6½″ squares for the foundation of all the appliqué blocks. Refer to the following appliqué block diagrams as a guide for appliqué and lettering placement. Make the number of blocks indicated for each. Lightly trace the lettering using the appliqué block text on pattern pullout page P3.

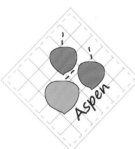

Aspen Leaf block—make 3.

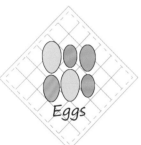

Bird Eggs block—make 2.

Butterfly block—make 3.

Coneflower block—make 3.

Deer Footprint block—make 2.

Dragonfly block—make 2.

Rabbit Footprint block—make 2.

Red Fox Footprint block—make 2.

Wild Rose block—make 3.

Willow Leaf block—make 2.

Embroidery

Use 3 strands of various shades of brown or green embroidery floss to backstitch the lettering and dot the *i*'s with French knots. We used 3 strands of brown embroidery floss and a backstitch for the butterfly antennae, 3 strands of green embroidery floss and a backstitch for the aspen leaf stems, 6 strands of green embroidery floss and a split stitch for the willow leaf stems, and 6 strands of green embroidery floss and a running stitch for the coneflower stems.

Wild Rose Centers

1. Gather the pale pink ½"-wide bias strip by sewing a basting stitch down the center.

2. Pull up the basting stitches until the strip measures 4½".

3. Sew over the basting stitches with a regular machine stitch.

4. Wind the gathered strip into a rosette shape.

5. Pin the rosette to the center of the rose and sew in place, taking care to sew in the center of the strip as much as possible.

6. Use your fingers to fluff and lightly fray the edges of the ruffle.

QUILT CENTER ASSEMBLY

1. Refer to the quilt layout diagram and assemble the quilt center by joining Nine-Patch blocks, appliqué blocks, plain peach blocks, corner triangles, and setting triangles in diagonal rows.

Note: The setting triangles are cut to extend or float beyond the points of the blocks to allow for variations in block size.

2. After top is assembled, straighten the sides of the quilt using a long ruler, and then square the corners, making sure to maintain a ¼" seam allowance at outside points.

BORDERS

Refer to Borders (page 103) to add the cream 6½" × 77" strips to the sides of the quilt. Use the cream 6½" × 72" strips for the top and bottom of the quilt.

QUILTING

Nancy Janikowsky machine quilted a very beautiful continuous wildflower design in the border with a smaller version in the plain peach blocks. She shadow-quilted the appliqués and added a sweet double leaf to each square in the Nine-Patch blocks.

BINDING

Referring to Binding (page 104), bind the quilt with the 2¼"-wide bias strip.

Quilt layout diagram

meadow path bed skirt

Designed and made by Susan Maw

FINISHED BED SKIRT: *Twin size with a 14″ or 19″ drop*

Our bed skirt adds a sweet, feminine touch to the Meadow Path bedroom set.

MATERIALS

- **White:** 5 yards for bed skirt with 14″ drop *or* 6¼ yards for bed skirt with 19″ drop

- **Orange plaid:** ⅝ yard for the contrast trim

- **Bleached muslin:** 2¼ yards for the platform

✦ CUTTING

Refer to General Sewing Instructions (page 108).

White:

- Cut 9 panels 14″ × width of fabric for the flounce for 14″ drop *or* 9 panels 19″ × width of fabric for 19″ drop.

- Cut 15 strips 3″ × width of fabric.

Orange plaid:

- Cut 9 strips 2″ × width of fabric.

Bleached muslin:

- Cut 1 panel 40″ × 76″ for the platform. To round the 2 corners of the platform that will be at the foot of the bed, place a piece of heavy paper between the mattress and box spring. Trace the shape of the corners. Use this paper as a template to round off each of the 2 corners.

✦ SEWING

A ½″ seam allowance is included in the pattern pieces unless otherwise noted.

1. Stitch the short sides of the flounce panels together to make a long unit. Finish the seams with a zigzag or overlock stitch, or trim with pinking shears. Press the seams open.

2. Stitch the short ends of the 9 orange plaid strips together to make a long strip. Press the seams open. Fold and lightly press the strip in half lengthwise, wrong sides together. Open out the fold and turn both edges in to meet the crease. Unfold and press the center fold flat.

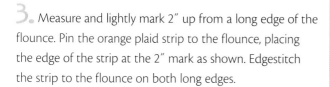

3. Measure and lightly mark 2″ up from a long edge of the flounce. Pin the orange plaid strip to the flounce, placing the edge of the strip at the 2″ mark as shown. Edgestitch the strip to the flounce on both long edges.

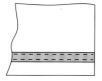

4. Stitch the ends of the 15 ruffle strips together to make a long strip. Press the seams open. Fold and press the strip in half lengthwise, wrong sides together. Gather the unfinished doubled edge with a ½″ seam allowance. (Gathering note: Divide the ruffle into 4 equal sections and mark it with pins before sewing in the gathering. Break stitching at the marks, leaving thread tails long. Divide the lower edge of the flounce in the same manner.) Pin the ruffle to the flounce, matching the division marks and pulling up basting stitches to fit. Stitch. Finish the seam by zigzagging, overlocking, or pinking. Press the seam toward the flounce. Topstitch ⅛″ from the seam.

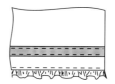

5. Gather the upper edge of the flounce, breaking the stitching at the panel seamlines. Mark the platform every 21″ from the top edge all the way around to the other top edge. Pin the flounce to the platform, placing the seams at the markings on the platform. Pull up basting stitches to fit. Stitch. Finish the seam. Press toward the platform.

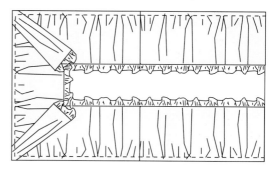

6. Press the platform, flounce, and ruffle under ½″ on the unfinished end. Open out the fold and turn under the raw edge to meet the crease. Press. Refold and stitch the hem in place.

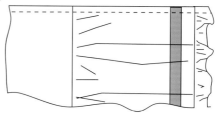

meadow path pillow sham

Designed and made by Susan Maw

FINISHED PILLOW SHAM: *Standard pillow size, 20″ × 26″, excluding 1″ ruffle*

FINISHED BLOCK: *6″ × 6″*

A sweet 1″ ruffle matches the Meadow Path bed skirt (page 68) and adds to the whole Meadow Path bedroom theme.

MATERIALS

- **White:** 1½ yards for the front, back, and ruffle

- **Cream tone-on-tone:** ⅓ yard for the appliqué blocks and inner sashing

- **Orange plaid:** ⅛ yard for the outer sashing

- **Blocks:** 1 square 5⅛″ × 5⅛″ each of 2 different pink fabrics and 2 different orange fabrics for the corner triangles

- **Assorted scraps:** Brown, purples, and pinks for appliqué pieces*

- **Embroidery floss** in brown and green

We made our pillow sham using the Coneflower and Wild Rose template pattern, but you may substitute any of the appliqué designs from the Meadow Path Quilt project (page 62), so your scrap colors may vary according to the designs you select.

CUTTING

The appliqué template and embroidery patterns are on pattern pullout pages P3 and P4. Note that the patterns are printed on both sides of the pullout, so you must trace and make your own templates. Cut the number of pieces needed for your selected blocks. Refer to General Sewing Instructions (page 108) and General Quiltmaking Instructions (page 102).

White:

- Cut 2 panels 19¼″ × 21″.
- Cut 2 strips 4½″ × 27″.
- Cut 2 strips 3¼″ × 13″.
- Cut 5 strips 3″ × width of fabric.

Cream tone-on-tone:

- Cut 2 squares 6½″ × 6½″.
- Cut 2 strips 1½″ × 11″.
- Cut 2 strips 1½″ × 17½″.

Orange plaid:

- Cut 2 strips 1½″ × 13″.
- Cut 2 strips 1½″ × 19½″.

Pinks and oranges:

- Cut each of the 4 squares 5⅛″ × 5⅛″ in half on the diagonal once for a total of 8 corner triangles.

- Cut 1 bias strip ½″ × 9″ from pale pink if you are making the Wild Rose appliqué block.

APPLIQUÉ

1. Refer to Raw-Edge Appliqué (page 103) in General Quiltmaking Instructions and *Meadow Path Quilt* appliqué layouts (page 66) to appliqué the design. If you are making the Wild Rose appliqué block, refer to Wild Rose Centers (page 67). Use the cream tone-on-tone 6½″ squares for the foundation of the appliqué blocks.

2. To finish the blocks, piece pink and orange corner triangles to each side of the appliqué blocks, using ¼″ seams. Blocks will measure 9″ square unfinished. Press toward the appliqué block. Stitch the appliquéd blocks together.

✦ SEWING

A ¼" seam allowance is included in the pattern pieces unless otherwise noted. Follow the arrows or written instructions for pressing direction.

1. Add the borders surrounding the appliqué blocks as shown in the diagram. For the first border use the cream 1½" strips, and for the second use the orange plaid 1½" strips. For the outside border, use the white 3¼" × 13" strips for the sides and the white 4½" × 27" strips for the top and bottom.

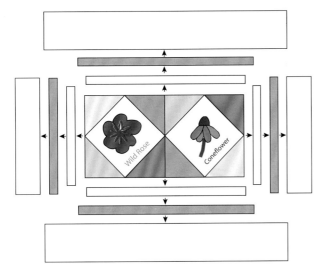

2. Stitch the ends of the 5 ruffle strips together to make a continuous circular strip. Press the seams open. Fold and press the strip in half lengthwise, wrong sides together. Gather the unfinished edge with a ½" seam allowance. Refer to Gathering Note, Step 4 (page 69). Pin the ruffle to the sham, matching the division marks and pulling up basting stitches to fit. Baste with a ½" seam allowance.

3. Using both white 19¼" × 21" pieces, press under 2" on a 21" side of each piece. Unfold and press under ½". Refold and stitch close to the pressed edge.

4. Pin the sham back panels to the sham front, with right sides together, overlapping the finished edges of the back to fit the front. Stitch with a ½" seam allowance, keeping the ruffle free. Trim the corners. Turn the sham right side out. Press. Insert a pillow.

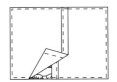

FUN IDEA!
Trim for sheets

Fun idea! When you are making the ruffles for the bed skirt or sham, make additional ruffles to add to a bed sheet to complete the Meadow Path bedroom set.

butterfly pillow

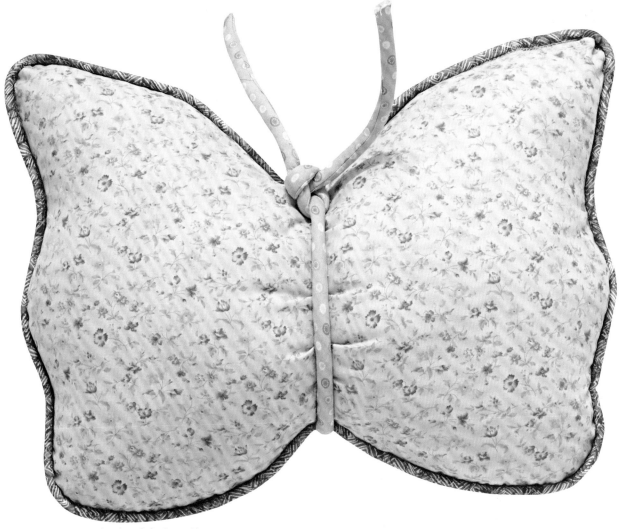

Designed and made by Susan Maw

FINISHED PILLOW: *18″ × 13″*

This butterfly floats across the room and lands
on the Meadow Path bedroom set!

MATERIALS

- **Yellow print:** ½ yard for the pillow front and back

- **Pink print:** 12″ × 12″ square for the pillow edge piping *or* 1 package bias corded piping

- **Aqua print:** 10½″ × 10½″ square for covered cording for the butterfly body

- **⁶⁄₃₂″-diameter piping cording:** 2 yards for the pillow edge (This cording isn't necessary if you're using packaged piping.)

- **¹²⁄₃₂″-diameter piping cording:** 2½ yards for the butterfly body

- **Polyester fiberfill**

CUTTING

Locate the Butterfly Pillow pattern on pattern pullout page P4. Note that the patterns are printed on both sides of the pullout, so refer to General Sewing Instructions (page 108) to prepare tissue paper patterns and for sewing tips. Cutting instructions are on each pattern piece. Label each cut pattern piece with the pattern letter and transfer any pattern markings.

Pink print:

- Refer to Continuous Bias Binding (page 105) in General Quiltmaking Instructions to make a bias fabric strip to cover the cording for the pillow edge, using the 12″ square. Cut the strip 1⅝″ wide.

Aqua print:

- Refer to Continuous Bias Binding (page 105) in General Quiltmaking Instructions to make a bias fabric strip to cover the cording for the butterfly, using the 10½″ square. Cut the strip 2⅛″ wide.

⚜ SEWING

A ½" seam allowance is included in the pattern pieces unless otherwise noted.

1. Make the pink piping for the edge of the pillow. With the sewing machine's zipper foot aligned to the left of the needle, center the 2 yards of ⁶⁄₃₂"-diameter cording on the wrong side of the bias strip, fold the strip over the cording, aligning the edges, and baste with the cord to the right of the needle.

2. Pin the piping to the right side of the pillow front, aligning the raw edges. Start the piping at the bottom center of the butterfly. Position the zipper foot to the right of the needle and baste over the previous stitching with the cord to the left of the needle, leaving the first ½" free of stitching. End the piping by overlapping the ends of the bias strip by ½", with the finishing end turned to the inside before overlapping. Cut the cording inside the pink fabric so that the ends butt together, and finish basting.

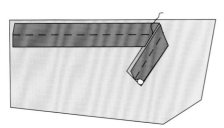

3. Continue to use the zipper foot to stitch the pillow front to the pillow back, leaving an opening to turn. Clip curves. Turn the pillow right side out.

4. Stuff the butterfly firmly, flattening as you stuff. You don't want the pillow to get too thick from front to back. Slipstitch the opening closed.

5. Make the covered cord for the butterfly body, using the aqua bias strip and the 2½ yards of ¹²⁄₃₂"-diameter cording. Wrap the bias strip wrong side out around the cord, placing the beginning of the bias at the center point of the cord. Use the machine's zipper foot and align the cording to the left of the needle. Sew across the end of the strip, sewing through the cord and for a couple of stitches past it. Pivot and stitch next to the cord to the end of the bias strip. Trim the seam allowance.

Pivot point

6. Turn the bias strip right side out over the cording by beginning where you started stitching and easing the bias strip gently over itself toward the exposed cording. Trim the excess cording. At the opposite end, turn the edge of the bias strip inside and stitch across the cording and bias strip. Trim the excess cording.

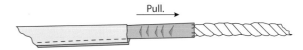

Pull.

7. Wrap the covered cording around the center of the butterfly pillow, slightly pulling in the pillow, and tie the ends at the top center. Position the ends up and out for the butterfly antennae.

woodland trail

Woodland Trail Quilt

Campy Kids Pillow

Woodland Trail Floor Rug

grizzly

woodland trail quilt

Designed by Sally Bell; pieced by Marie Lanier; quilted by Jennine Jones

FINISHED QUILT: *72″ × 84″*

FINISHED BEAR FOOT BLOCK: *6″ × 6″*

FINISHED TEEPEE BLOCK: *10″ × 12″*

FINISHED FISH BLOCK: *6″ × 4″*

Our *Woodland Trail Quilt* brings the outdoors inside with trees, bears, and fish. After a busy day of hiking and exploring, sleepyheads will love to crawl under this beauty and dream of their wonderful day.

MATERIALS

- **Blues/aquas (referred to as blues):** ¼ yard each of 27 different prints

- **Greens:** ¼ yard each of 12 different prints

- **Browns:** ¼ yard each of 6 different prints

- **Reds:** 1 fat quarter each of 5 different prints

- **Purple:** ⅛ yard

- **Yellow:** ⅛ yard

- **Backing:** 5 yards

- **Batting:** 78″ × 90″

- **Binding:** ⅞ yard

- **Embroidery floss:** black

🐾 CUTTING

Locate the Woodland Trail Quilt *template patterns A–L on pattern pullout pages P2–P4. Note that the patterns are printed on both sides of the pullout, so you must trace the patterns to make your own templates to preserve the original pullout. Cutting instructions are on each pattern piece. Label each cut template and fabric piece with the letter and/or quilt block name. Refer to General Quiltmaking Instructions (page 102).*

Blues:

▪ Cut 1 strip 6½″ × width of fabric; subcut into 4 squares 6½″ × 6½″ (solid blocks).

▪ Cut 1 strip 6¼″ × width of fabric; subcut into 2 squares 6¼″ × 6¼″. Cut these in half on the diagonal twice to make 8 corner triangles (Corner Tree block).

▪ Cut 1 strip 4½″ × width of fabric; subcut into 3 rectangles 4½″ × 6½″ (Fish blocks).

▪ Cut 19 strips 3½″ × width of fabric; subcut into 208 squares 3½″ × 3½″ (88 for Bear Foot block, 40 for Tree block, 80 for Flying Geese block).

▪ Cut 6 strips 3″ × width of fabric; subcut into 10 rectangles 3″ × 6½″ (Tree Trunk block) and 40 rectangles 3″ × 3½″ (Tree block).

▪ Cut 18 strips 2½″ × width of fabric; subcut into 6 rectangles 2½″ × 10½″ (Teepee block) and 144 squares 2½″ × 2½″ (Lake section).

▪ Cut 2 strips 2″ × width of fabric; subcut into 20 rectangles 2″ × 3″ (Triple Tree block).

▪ Cut 9 strips 1⅞″ × width of fabric; subcut into 176 squares 1⅞″ × 1⅞″ (Bear Foot block).

▪ Cut 4 strips 1½″ × width of fabric; subcut into 88 squares 1½″ × 1½″ (Bear Foot block).

Greens:

▪ Cut 1 strip 6⅞″ × width of fabric; subcut into 2 squares 6⅞″ × 6⅞″. Cut in half on the diagonal to make 4 corner triangles (Corner Tree block).

▪ Cut 4 strips 6½″ × width of fabric; subcut into 23 squares 6½″ × 6½″ (solid blocks).

▪ Cut 10 strips 3½″ × width of fabric; subcut into 60 rectangles 3½″ × 6½″ (20 for Tree block, 40 for Flying Geese block).

Browns:

▪ Cut 6 strips 2½″ × width of fabric; subcut into 88 squares 2½″ × 2½″ (Bear Foot block).

▪ Cut 1 strip 2″ × width of fabric; subcut into 4 rectangles 2″ × 5″ (Corner Tree block).

▪ Cut 9 strips 1⅞″ × width of fabric; subcut into 176 squares 1⅞″ × 1⅞″ (Bear Foot block).

▪ Cut 4 strips 1½″ × width of fabric; subcut into 5 rectangles 1½″ × 6½″ (Tree Trunk block), 20 rectangles 1½″ × 3½″ (Tree block), and 10 rectangles 1½″ × 2″ (Triple Tree block).

Binding:

▪ Cut 1 square 28″ × 28″. Refer to Continuous Bias Binding (page 105) in General Quiltmaking Instructions to make 325″ of bias strip 2¼″ wide.

✦ BLOCK ASSEMBLY

Refer to General Quiltmaking Instructions (page 102). Use a ¼" seam allowance. Follow the arrows for pressing direction.

Bear Foot Block

1. Refer to Half-Square Triangles (page 107) in General Quiltmaking Instructions. Use all the blue and brown 1⅞" squares to piece 352 half-square triangle units, finished size 1". Press the seams toward the browns.

2. Use 2 brown/blue units from Step 1 and a brown 2½" square to piece Unit 1 as shown.

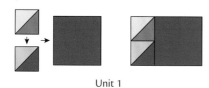

Unit 1

3. Use a blue 1½" square and 2 brown/blue units from Step 1 to piece Unit 2 as shown.

Unit 2

4. Use Unit 1 and Unit 2 to piece Unit 3 as shown. Repeat Steps 2–4 to make a total of 88 of Unit 3.

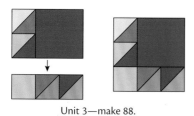

Unit 3—make 88.

5. Use 1 blue 3½" square and 1 Unit 3 to piece Unit 4 as shown. Make a total of 44 of Unit 4.

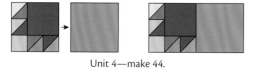

Unit 4—make 44.

6. Use 1 blue 3½" square and 1 Unit 3 to piece Unit 4r as shown. Make a total of 44 Units 4r.

Unit 4r—make 44.

7. Sew Units 4 and 4r together in pairs to yield the block as shown. Complete a total of 44 Bear Foot blocks.

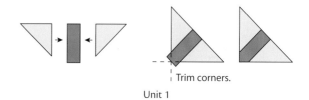

Bear Foot block—make 44.

Corner Tree Block

1. For Unit 1, sew a blue triangle to each side of a brown 2" × 5" rectangle, matching at the tops. Use an acrylic ruler to square up the bottom corner and trim off the brown rectangle. Repeat to make 4 units.

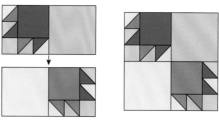

Trim corners.

Unit 1

2. Sew Unit 1 to a green 6⅞" × 6⅞" half-square triangle to complete the block. Repeat to make a total of 4.

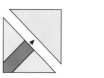

Corner Tree block—make 4.

Tree Trunk Block

Sew a blue 3″ × 6½″ rectangle to each side of a brown 1½″ × 6½″ rectangle. Make a total of 5 Tree Trunk blocks.

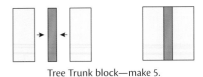

Tree Trunk block—make 5.

Tree Block

1. Sew a blue 3″ × 3½″ rectangle to each side of a brown 1½″ × 3½″ rectangle to make Unit 1. Repeat to make 20.

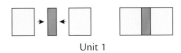

Unit 1

2. Refer to Flying Geese (page 106) in General Quiltmaking Instructions. Piece 20 Flying Geese units 3½″ × 6½″ from the greens and blues.

3. Sew Unit 1 to a Flying Geese unit to complete the block. Make a total of 20 Tree blocks.

Tree block—make 20.

Flying Geese Block

1. Refer to Flying Geese (page 106) in General Quiltmaking Instructions. Piece 40 Flying Geese units 3½″ × 6½″, using 40 green 3½″ × 6½″ pieces and 80 blue 3½″ squares.

2. Sew 2 Flying Geese units together to complete the block. Make a total of 20 Flying Geese blocks.

Flying Geese block—make 20.

Triple Tree Block

1. For Unit 1, sew a blue 2″ × 3″ rectangle to each side of a brown 1½″ × 2″ rectangle.

Unit 1

2. Use a blue Template D, a green Template C, and a blue Template C to make Unit 2.

Unit 2

3. Use a blue Template Dr, a green Template C, and a blue Template C to make Unit 2r.

Unit 2r

4. Sew a blue Template B to Unit 2 to yield Unit 3.

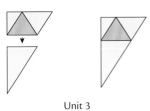

Unit 3

5. Sew a blue Template Br to Unit 2r to yield Unit 3r.

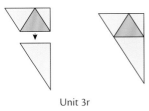

Unit 3r

6. Sew a Unit 3 and a Unit 3r to a green Template A to make Unit 4.

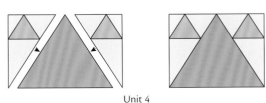

Unit 4

7. Sew Unit 1 to Unit 4 to piece the block. Repeat Steps 1–7 to make 10 Triple Tree blocks.

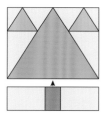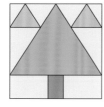

Triple-Tree block—make 10.

Teepee Block

Note: The Teepee block uses matching fabric sets of F, H, and Hr for each block.

1. Use a red Template H, a red Template Hr, and a red Template G to make Unit 1.

Unit 1

2. Sew a red Template F to Unit 1 to yield Unit 2.

Unit 2

3. Sew a blue Template E and a blue Template Er to Unit 2 to yield Unit 3.

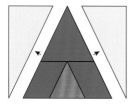

Unit 3

4. Sew a blue 2½″ × 10½″ rectangle to Unit 3 to piece the block. Repeat Steps 1–4 to make 6 Teepee blocks.

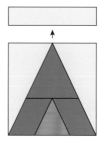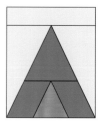

Teepee block—make 6.

Fish Blocks

1. Refer to Raw-Edge Appliqué (page 103) in General Quiltmaking Instructions.

2. Fold a blue 4½″ × 6½″ rectangle in half horizontally. Finger-press the fold. Open out the fabric. Center the fish and tail on the rectangle using the fold line as a guide.

3. Appliqué the Fish Tail I and Fish J in place. Make a red fish block, a yellow fish block, and a purple fish block.

Fish block—make 3.

Bears

1. Refer to Raw-Edge Appliqué (page 103) in General Quiltmaking Instructions.

2. Appliqué K and L bears in place as indicated on the quilt layout diagram (page 84).

QUILT ASSEMBLY

Refer to the quilt layout diagram to assemble the quilt. Note that Bear Foot blocks are turned to look like they "walk" around the quilt. (Suggestion: Sew the 144 blue 2½" squares with the 3 Fish blocks. Then proceed with piecing the top together, following the quilt layout.)

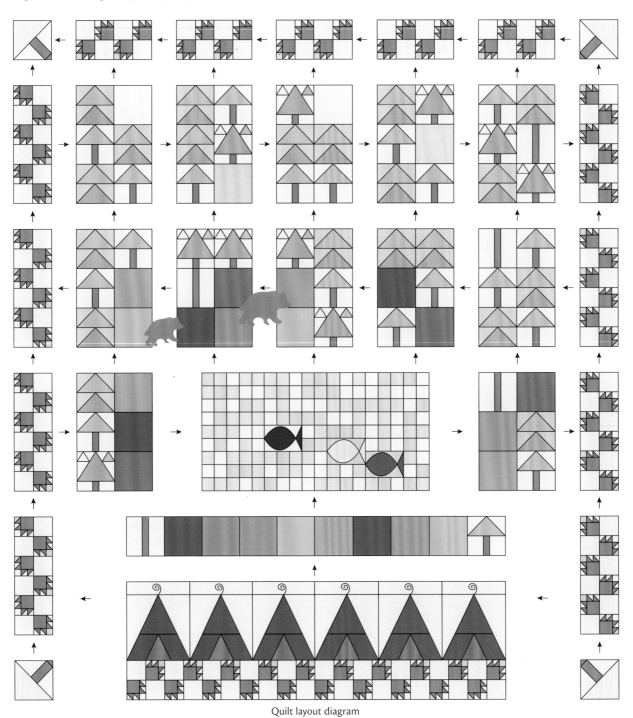

Quilt layout diagram

🐾 EMBROIDERY

1. Refer to Embroidery Stitches (page 109) in General Sewing Instructions.

2. Use a backstitch to embroider smoke swirling from the tops of the teepees.

🐾 QUILTING

Jennine Jones quilted lots of swirls throughout the quilt. She detailed the trees with curves to indicate pine boughs; she quilted a reflective design in the lake to replicate water. She even quilted fur on the bears and scales on the fish!

🐾 BINDING

Refer to Binding (page 104) in General Quiltmaking Instructions.

Campy Kids Pillow

Designed and made by Sally Bell

FINISHED PILLOW: *16" square + 2" fringe*

I remember going to Yellowstone National Park with my family when I was about six years old. My sisters and I each got a pink satin pillowcase with a map of Yellowstone Park printed on it and fringe around the edge. I loved that pillowcase. I don't know where it is now, but I'm sure it would be a vintage treasure. By using satin and fringe to make this pillow, we've created a project that takes us back to our childhood.

CUTTING

Locate the Campy Kids Pillow template pattern pieces A–C on pattern pullout pages P2–P4. Note that the patterns are printed on both sides of the pullout. To preserve the original pullouts, trace the patterns to make your own templates. Cutting instructions are on each pattern piece. Label each cut template with the letter. Refer to the General Sewing Instructions (page 108).

Satin:

- Cut 1 square 17″ × 17″ for the pillow front.

- Cut 1 rectangle 9″ × 17″ for the pillow lower back.

- Cut 1 rectangle 12″ × 17″ for the pillow upper back.

Interfacing:

- Cut 1 square 17″ × 17″.

MATERIALS

- **Satin:** ½ yard

- **Cording:** 4 yards for *Campy*; 2 yards for *kids*

- **Scraps of wool:** for tree and bears

- **Fringe:** 2 yards

- **Pillow form:** 16″

- **Fusible interfacing:** ½ yard (for example, Shape-Flex)

- **Paper-backed fusible web, 20″ wide:** 12″ × 12″ piece

- **Button:** 1″ diameter

PILLOW CONSTRUCTION

A ½" seam is included in the pattern pieces unless otherwise noted.

1. Following the manufacturer's directions, fuse the interfacing to the back side of the pillow front.

2. Refer to the pillow layout for *Campy kids* words, tree, and bear placement.

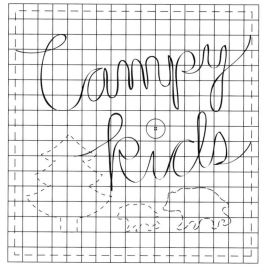

Pillow layout

3. Work by hand with needle and thread to couch the cording onto the pillow, following the transferred lines. The ends of the *Campy* cording should start and end in the seam allowance. The *kids* cording should start on the left where the tree will be appliquéd and end in the seam allowance on the right. Sew back and forth several times over the ends so that they will not fray or come loose.

4. Transfer the wool appliqués to the pillow at the placement lines, using the manufacturer's directions for the paper-backed fusible web. Blanket stitch around the appliqués by machine or by hand.

5. To attach the fringe to the pillow, pin it to the right side of the pillow front, aligning the outside edges and starting and ending at the bottom center of the pillow. Clip fringe at the corners. Baste, pivoting at the corners.

6. Turn under ½" on a long edge of each pillow back piece. Press. Repeat. Stitch.

7. Align the pillow back lower rectangle to the pillow front, right sides together, matching bottom unfinished edges.

8. Align the pillow back upper rectangle to the pillow front, right sides together, matching top unfinished edges and overlapping lower rectangle with the upper piece.

9. Sew around the pillow perimeter, pivoting at the corners.

10. Turn right side out. Press, sew the button on the pillow front to dot the *i*, and insert a pillow form.

woodland trail floor rug

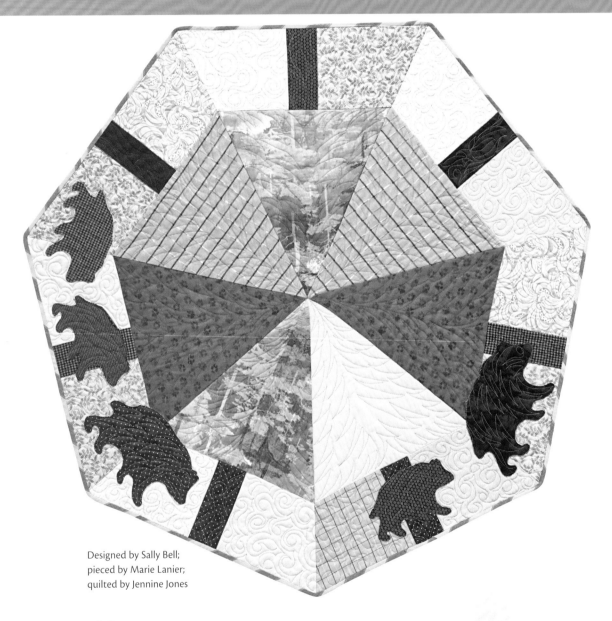

Designed by Sally Bell;
pieced by Marie Lanier;
quilted by Jennine Jones

FINISHED RUG: *40" diameter*

Complete the woodland trail theme in your
little one's bedroom with this small floor rug.
It emulates the *Woodland Trail Quilt* and warms
those little feet in the crisp mountain mornings.

MATERIALS

- **Greens:** 7 fat quarters in a mix of green prints (We used 4 different prints.)

- **Blues/aquas (referred to as blues):** ¼ yard each of 4 different prints

- **Browns:** ¼ yard each of 2 different prints

- **Backing:** 1⅓ yards (at least 44″ wide or you will need more)

- **Batting:** 44″ × 44″

- **Binding:** ⅝ yard

Optional:

- **Nonslip rug pad:** 40″ × 40″, if using the rug on a slippery floor

CUTTING

Locate the Woodland Trail Rug template patterns (small and large bears) on pattern pullout pages P3 and P4. Note that the patterns are printed on both sides of the pullout. To preserve the original pullouts, trace the patterns to make your own templates. Cutting instructions are on each template piece. Label each cut template with the letter. Refer to General Sewing Instructions (page 108).

Greens:

Refer to Woodland Trail Rug Tree A cutting diagram.

1. Use 7 green fat quarters. Square up the fat quarters.

2. Refer to the Woodland Trail Rug A cutting diagram to measure and mark the fabric with the 2 dots along the bottom edge of each fat quarter. Then measure and mark the dot at the apex of the triangle, as indicated on the cutting diagram. Draw the cutting lines shown.

3. Cut 7 Woodland Trail Rug Tree A pieces by cutting on the lines.

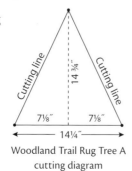

Woodland Trail Rug Tree A
cutting diagram

Blues:

1. From each blue fabric: Cut 1 strip 6″ × width of fabric; subcut into 4 pieces 6″ × 9″ for a total of 16 pieces. (You'll only use 14.)

2. Refer to the Woodland B/Br cutting diagram. Arrange 7 blue 6″ × 9″ pieces right side up. Measure and mark only the red B dot indicated in the diagram on the top edge of each fabric piece. Draw a cutting line (shown in red) from the dot to the lower left corner of the piece. Cut these B pieces.

3. Again refer to the Woodland B/Br cutting diagram. Arrange 7 blue 6″ × 9″ pieces right side up. Measure and mark only the black Br dot indicated in the diagram on the top edge of each fabric piece. Draw a cutting line (shown in black) from the dot to the lower right corner of the piece. Cut these Br pieces.

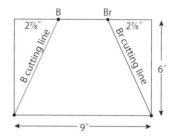

Woodland Trail Rug B/Br cutting diagram

Browns:

- Cut 1 strip 3″ × width of fabric; subcut into a total of 7 rectangles 3″ × 6″.

Binding:

- Cut 1 square 18½″ × 18½″. Refer to Curved Bias Binding (page 105). You will need approximately 150″ of bias strip, cut 1½″ wide.

🐾 BLOCK ASSEMBLY

Follow the arrows for pressing direction. A ¼" seam is included in the pattern pieces unless otherwise noted.

1. Use a blue piece B, a blue piece Br, and a brown rectangle to make Unit 1.

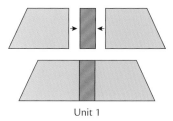

Unit 1

2. Sew a green piece A to Unit 1 to complete Unit 2. Repeat Steps 1 and 2 to make 7 sections.

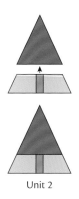

Unit 2

🐾 RUG ASSEMBLY

Sew 7 units together to complete the rug.

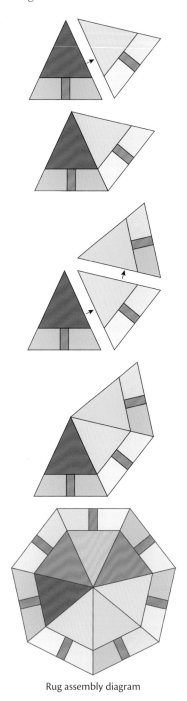

Rug assembly diagram

Bears

Refer to Raw-Edge Appliqué (page 103) in General Quiltmaking Instructions. Appliqué the 5 bears in place as indicated in the rug photo.

🐾 QUILTING

Jennine Jones emulated pine boughs in the trees and bark in the tree trunks. She continued with swirls in the blue sections.

🐾 BINDING

Use the 1½"-wide bias strip as binding. Refer to Curved Bias Binding (page 105) in General Quiltmaking Instructions.

fun things to do

crow

Campy Kids Finger Puppets

Popcorn Packs

Gooey Peanut Butter
S'Mores

My Treasure Box

Animal Tracks
Reference Cards

campy kids finger puppets

Finger puppets! What a fun way to play and learn about animals. Kids will love playing with these.

☀ SUPPLIES

- White card stock: 8½″ × 11″ sheet
- Scissors
- Scotch tape

☀ INSTRUCTIONS

Photocopy the puppets onto white card stock. Cut them out, clipping on the dotted lines. Wrap the puppet around your child's finger and tape tab over tab.

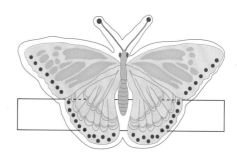

popcorn packs

INGREDIENTS

- 1 piece of aluminum foil, 10″ square
- 1 teaspoon cooking oil
- 1 tablespoon popcorn kernels
- Salt, if desired

RECIPE

1. Place the oil and popcorn kernels in the center of the foil square.

2. Pull the corners of the foil up and to the middle, and twist, sealing the pack with your fingers.

3. Twist the "ears" of the foil around a roaster stick and place on the coals in the campfire or on the grill.

4. Shake periodically until the kernels have finished popping.

5. Open carefully.

6. Salt, if desired.

(Don't forget to leave some on the ground for the birds!)

Kids don't need to be at the movie theater to enjoy popcorn! What a special treat when they can pop their own popcorn right over the campfire.

gooey peanut butter s'mores

INGREDIENTS

- Large marshmallows
- Miniature peanut butter cups
- Graham crackers

RECIPE

1. Put a marshmallow on a stick and roast it over the campfire or grill.

2. Break a graham cracker in half across the middle.

3. Place a peanut butter cup on a graham cracker half.

4. When the marshmallow is roasted to golden brown, place it on top of the graham cracker half that has the peanut butter cup, place the other half of the graham cracker on top of the marshmallow, and "smush" it together as you pull the marshmallow off the stick with the crackers.

5. Yum, yum!

Peanut butter, chocolate, marshmallows, and graham crackers! That covers everything on a kid's goody list. And it's an all-in-one treat! Wow, there's nothing else to say.

my treasure box

SUPPLIES

- Small cardboard box with lid
- Printed paper and coordinating ribbon or jute cord
- Small charm
- Glue

INSTRUCTIONS

1. Cover the box and lid with paper.

2. Fill the box with treasures found in your yard or at the park: leaves, rocks, feathers, flowers, and so on.

3. Wrap the box and lid with a special ribbon or cord and add a special charm.

What kid doesn't cherish a secret box filled with a personal cache of treasures found on hikes and special outings? Just open the lid and enjoy all the magical memories of days gone by.

animal tracks reference cards

Kids love animals. Finding and cataloging animal tracks is a great learning project, but don't tell the kids!

SUPPLIES

- White card stock: 8½″ × 11″ sheet
- Scissors
- Hole punch
- 1″ loose-leaf ring

INSTRUCTIONS

1. Enlarge the tags 200% and photocopy them onto white card stock and cut them out.

2. Punch out a hole and put the tags on a loose-leaf ring.

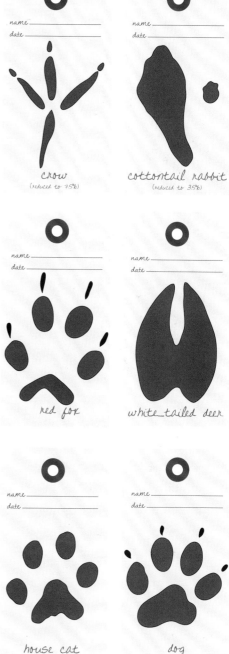

name _____
date _____

crow
(reduced to 75%)

name _____
date _____

cottontail rabbit
(reduced to 35%)

name _____
date _____

red fox

name _____
date _____

white tailed deer

name _____
date _____

house cat

name _____
date _____

dog

general quiltmaking instructions

Please read all instructions before beginning a project.

SEAM ALLOWANCES

Use ¼" seam allowances unless otherwise noted.

FABRIC

We use high-quality 100% cotton fabric purchased from our local quilt store or a specialized quilt store on the Internet. Fabric purchased from discount stores will not give you the same appearance as the quilts pictured. We don't wash and dry fabric before using it, because we like the feel of the fabric with the sizing left in it for piecing and sewing. After finishing a quilt, we wash and dry it. We like the look we get with a bit of shrinkage to "age" the quilt. However, if you are concerned about some fabrics bleeding, especially reds, yellows, and greens, then prewashing is a must. Also, for heavily appliquéd quilts or those with wool appliqué, it is best to prewash.

NEEDLES AND THREAD

We use 50-weight all-cotton thread with a size 70 needle for machine piecing, and a 50- or 60-weight all-cotton machine embroidery thread with a size 70 needle for machine appliqué.

APPLIQUÉ

Machine Appliqué

There are many different methods to use for machine appliqué. We use freezer paper and starch. If you have a favorite method, then use what you are comfortable with.

Freezer-Paper-and-Starch Method

1. Trace the appliqué template onto the shiny side of the freezer paper using a fine-point permanent pen or marker. Cut it out. (Do not add a seam allowance to the template.) Iron this piece to the dull side of a second piece of freezer paper. This gives you a stronger template.

2. Iron the freezer-paper template, shiny side down, to the wrong side of the fabric. Cut out the fabric pieces with a scant ¼" seam allowance. Clip the seam allowance at the inner points and around the curves, clipping a few threads shy of the freezer-paper template.

3. Spray some starch into a small bowl and allow the foam to disappear. Dip a small paintbrush into the starch and "paint" the seam allowance of the appliqué shape.

4. Press the seam allowance onto the freezer-paper template. Using a small iron, such as a Clover Mini Iron, makes this step easier. A stiletto helps turn curves smoothly and helps in making points sharp.

5. Remove the freezer-paper template and press from the top of the fabric. This template can be used again to create additional appliqués.

6. Arrange the appliqué shapes on the background fabric and baste them in place with a washable fabric glue. We prefer Roxanne Glue-Baste-It.

7. Machine stitch the shapes in place with a variable overlock or blind hem stitch, using thread to match the appliqué shape.

Raw-Edge Appliqué

1. Trace the appliqué template onto the dull side of the freezer paper using a fine-point permanent pen or marker. Cut it out. Do not add a seam allowance to the template.

2. Iron the shiny side of the freezer-paper template to the right side of the fabric. Cut the shape out. Do not add a seam allowance. Remove the freezer paper.

3. Arrange the appliqué shapes on the background fabric and baste them in place with a washable fabric glue. We prefer Roxanne Glue-Baste-It.

4. Machine stitch the shapes in place by sewing ⅛"–¼" from the raw edges. Use thread to match the appliqué shape and a straight stitch in a short length.

Wool Appliqué

We use overdyed wool that has been felted.

1. Trace the appliqué template onto the dull side of the freezer paper and cut the shape out. Do not add a seam allowance to the template.

2. Iron the shiny side of the freezer-paper template to the right side of the wool.

3. Cut the shape out. Do not add a seam allowance. Remove the freezer paper.

4. Arrange the appliqué shapes on the background and baste them in place with a washable fabric glue. We prefer Roxanne Glue-Baste-It.

5. Hand stitch the shapes in place with all-cotton thread or embroidery floss in a neutral color, using a whipstitch. Or machine stitch with a variable overlock or blind hem stitch.

SASHING

Measure through the center of the unfinished block to determine *your* actual measurement. This is the length to cut the sashing strips.

BORDERS

Butted Borders

In most cases the side borders are sewn on first. When you have finished the quilt top, measure it through the center vertically. This will be the length to cut the side borders. Place pins at the centers of all four sides of the quilt top, as well as in the center of each side border strip. Pin the side borders to the quilt top first, matching the center pins. Using a ¼" seam allowance, sew the borders to the quilt top and press toward the border.

Measure horizontally across the center of the quilt top, including the side borders. This will be the length to cut the top and bottom borders. Repeat, pinning, sewing, and pressing.

BACKING

Backing should be at least 6" longer and wider than the quilt top. Piece, if necessary, using leftover quilting fabrics.

BATTING

We prefer 100% cotton batting. Batting should be at least 6" longer and wider than the quilt top.

BINDING

Trim excess batting and backing from the quilt and square up the quilt.

Double-Fold Straight-Grain Binding

If you want a ¼" finished binding, cut the binding strips 2" wide and piece them together with diagonal seams to make a continuous binding strip. Trim the seam allowance to ¼". Press the seams open.

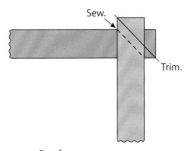

Sew from corner to corner.

Completed diagonal seam

Press the entire strip in half lengthwise with wrong sides together. With raw edges even, pin the binding to the front edge of the quilt a few inches away from a corner, and leave the first few inches of the binding unattached. Start sewing, using a ¼" seam allowance.

Stop ¼" away from the first corner (see Step 1), and back-stitch one stitch. Lift the presser foot and needle. Remove the quilt from the needle. Rotate the quilt one-quarter turn. Fold the binding at a right angle so it extends straight above the quilt and the fold forms a 45° angle in the corner (see Step 2). Then bring the binding strip down even with the edge of the quilt (see Step 3). Begin sewing at the folded edge. Repeat in the same manner at all corners.

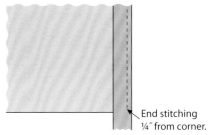

1. Stitch to ¼" from corner.

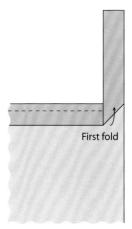

2. First fold for miter

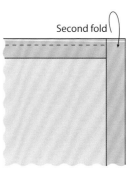

3. Second fold alignment

Continue stitching until you are back near the beginning of the binding strip. See Finishing the Binding Ends (page 106) for tips on finishing and hiding the raw edges of the ends of the binding.

Continuous Bias Binding

A continuous bias binding involves using a square of fabric sliced in half diagonally, and then sewing the resulting triangles together so that you continuously cut to make a single long strip on the bias. The same instructions can be used to cut bias for piping. Cut the fabric for the bias binding or piping so it is a square. For example, if yardage is ½ yard, cut an 18″ × 18″ square. Cut the square in half diagonally, creating two triangles.

Sew these triangles together as shown, using a ¼″ seam allowance. Press the seam open.

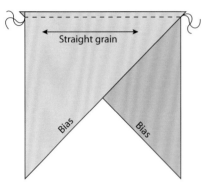

Sew triangles together.

Using a ruler, mark the parallelogram created by the two triangles with lines spaced the width you need to cut the bias. Cut about 5″ along the first line.

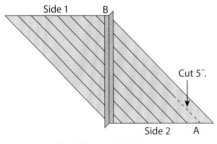

Mark lines and begin cut.

Join Side 1 and Side 2 to form a tube. The raw edge at point A will align with the raw edge at B. This will allow the first line to be offset by one strip width. Pin the raw edges right sides together, making sure that the drawn lines match. Sew with a ¼″ seam allowance. Press the seam open. Cut along the drawn lines, creating one continuous strip.

Press the entire strip in half lengthwise with wrong sides together. Place binding on quilt as described in Double-Fold Straight-Grain Binding (previous page).

See Finishing the Binding Ends for tips on finishing and hiding the raw edges of the ends of the binding.

Curved Bias Binding

Use a single thickness when applying binding to scallops or curved quilt edges. Cut bias strips 1½″ wide. Press one edge under ¼″. Pin the unpressed edge of the binding to the edge of the quilt top, right sides together. Stitch with a ¼″ seam allowance, easing the binding at the outer curves without stretching, and pivoting at the inner curves. Clip the seam allowances at the innermost point. Wrap the pressed edge of the binding around to the back of the quilt and hand stitch in place.

FINISHING THE BINDING ENDS

Method 1

After stitching around the quilt, fold under the beginning tail of the binding strip ¼″ so that the raw edge will be inside the binding after it is turned to the back of the quilt. Place the end tail of the binding strip over the beginning folded end. Continue to attach the binding and stitch slightly beyond the starting stitches. Trim the excess binding. Fold the binding over the raw edges to the quilt back and hand stitch, mitering the corners.

Method 2

See the tip "Completing a Binding with an Invisible Seam" at www.ctpub.com in the Consumer Resources section under Quiltmaking Basics.

Fold the ending tail of the binding back on itself where it meets the beginning binding tail. From the fold, measure and mark the cut width of the binding strip. Cut the ending binding tail to this measurement. For example, if the binding is cut 2⅛″ wide, measure from the fold on the ending tail of the binding 2⅛″ and cut the binding tail to this length.

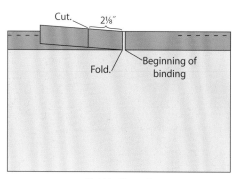

Cut binding tail.

Open both tails. Place one tail on top of the other tail at right angles, right sides together. Mark a diagonal line from corner to corner and stitch on the line. Check that you've done it correctly and that the binding fits the quilt; then trim the seam allowance to ¼″. Press open.

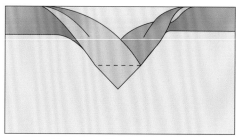

Stitch ends of binding diagonally.

Refold the binding and stitch this binding section in place on the quilt. Fold the binding over the raw edges to the quilt back and hand stitch.

FLYING GEESE

1. Lightly draw a diagonal line from a corner to the opposite corner on the wrong sides of 2 squares.

2. With right sides together, place a square on an end of the rectangle, as shown. Sew directly on the line, trim the seam allowance to ¼″, and press open.

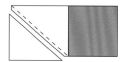

3. With right sides together, place the other square on the other end of the rectangle. Sew directly on the line, trim the seam allowance to ¼″, and press open.

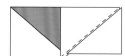

HALF-SQUARE TRIANGLES

1. Add ⅞" to the finished size of the unit and then cut a light and a dark square to that size. For example, if the finished size called for is 2", then cut the squares 2⅞".

2. Draw a diagonal line across the back of the light square and place it on the dark square, right sides together.

Draw line.

3. Sew ¼" from each side of the diagonal line.

Sew.

4. Cut the squares apart on the center line. You will have 2 half-square triangle units. Press toward the dark fabric.

FINALLY

We want to encourage your creativity. Don't be afraid to make our design your design. Most of all, have fun sewing and quilting!

general sewing instructions

1. Please read all instructions before beginning a project.

2. Take note of seam allowances on a per-project basis; they vary from ¼″ to ⅝″.

3. If you are using washable fabric for garment sewing, wash, dry, and press all fabric and trim before using.

4. Backstitch at the beginning and end of a seam by taking a few stitches in reverse to prevent the stitches from coming undone.

5. Clip the seam allowances at curves and corners.

6. Finish the seam allowances with a zigzag or overlock stitch, or trim with pinking shears.

7. Press the seams flat to set the stitches and then press them open unless otherwise noted.

CUTTING

1. Fold the fabric wrong sides together and align the selvage edges for double thickness; place right side up for single thickness.

2. Because the patterns are printed on both sides of the pullout pages, you must trace your own patterns and templates to preserve the original sheets intact. Mark the cutting lines for the size you want by tracing them with a highlighter before you trace your tissue paper patterns.

3. Arrange the pattern pieces before pinning them to the fabric to check the layout and to get the best use of the fabric. Note the grainline on the pattern pieces and align pattern arrows with the grain.

4. Transfer pattern markings to the wrong side of the fabric using a chalk pencil or removable pen.

Notches and symbols

5. Place right sides together when sewing pieces together unless otherwise noted.

6. When seams have multiple layers, grade seams by trimming the layers separately and into graded widths.

GLOSSARY OF SEWING TERMS

Backstitching: A few stitches sewn in reverse at the beginning and end of a seam to prevent the stitches from coming undone.

Basting stitch: The longest stitch available on a sewing machine, used mainly as a temporary stitch to keep multiple layers of fabric together.

Edge stitch: A straight stitch that runs close to a seam or finished edge and is stitched with the right side up.

Gathering: Two rows of basting stitches, one along the seamline and the other ¼″ inside the seam allowance. The bobbin threads of each set of stitches are pulled to gather the fabric and adjust the fullness evenly. After the gathered area has been sewn to the garment, the two rows of basting are removed.

Grainline: The straight grain of the fabric; the line parallel to the selvage or fold.

Slip stitch: A loose hand stitch that catches only a thread or two of fabric, designed to be invisible from the right side.

Stay stitch: A straight stitch, usually ½″ in from the cut edge, within the seam allowance, that prevents fabric from stretching.

Top stitch: A straight stitch that runs parallel usually ¼″ away from an edge or another seam and is stitched with the right side up.

SIZE CHART

	SIZE 3	SIZE 4	SIZE 5	SIZE 6	SIZE 7	SIZE 8
Chest	21½″	22½″	23½″	24″	25″	26″
Waist	20½″	21″	22″	22½″	23″	23½″
Hips	22″	23″	24¼″	25½″	26¾″	27½″
Height	38½″	41″	43½″	46″	48″	50½″

EMBROIDERY STITCHES

We like to use hand embroidery stitches to embellish our quilts.

1. Use an air- or water-soluble pen to draw the designs on the fabric.

2. Use size 5 perle cotton or 3 strands of embroidery floss, unless otherwise noted, and a size 5 embroidery needle.

3. When finishing, take the needle to the back and knot the thread or knot the thread first and hide it inside the work.

Stitch Guide

Backstitch

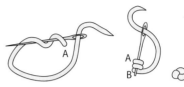

French knot

Running stitch

Split stitch

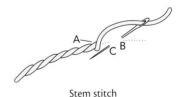

Stem stitch

Whipstitch

about the authors

Sally and Susan

Susan Maw and Sally Bell have created together since they were kids on their parents' farm using their cats as models for their doll clothes. They had a business together making dolls in the 1980s, and after taking a break to raise their families, they started their current business, Maw-Bell Designs. They love to create the look for each book and follow through with the designs that add to the theme. They love all aspects of art, but playing with color and fabric is the most rewarding.

Susan and her family live in northwestern Montana near beautiful Glacier National Park. She has three sons and a daughter. Sally and her family live in midwestern Montana in the mountains of the Bitterroot Valley. She has one son, one daughter, and one granddaughter. They feel so fortunate to be sisters who both enjoy designing, talking about designing, and redesigning after they have talked about design. *Sew a Backyard Adventure* is their second book for C&T.

Visit the Maw-Bell Designs website and blog (at right).

Also by Susan Maw and Sally Bell:

RESOURCES

Maw-Bell Designs
www.maw-belldesigns.com
www.maw-belldesigns.blogspot.com
email: info@maw-belldesigns.com
406-755-6263
406-360-1404

Prym Consumer USA Inc.
www.dritz.com
864-587-5270

Great Titles *from* FunStitch Studio & stashBOOKS.

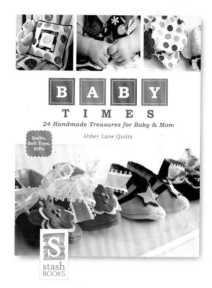

Available at your local retailer or **www.ctpub.com** *or* **800-284-1114**

For a list of other fine books from C&T Publishing, visit our website to view our catalog online.

C&T PUBLISHING, INC.

P.O. Box 1456
Lafayette, CA 94549
800-284-1114

Email: ctinfo@ctpub.com
Website: www.ctpub.com

C&T Publishing's professional photography services are now available to the public. Visit us at www.ctmediaservices.com.

Tips and Techniques can be found at www.ctpub.com > Consumer Resources > Quiltmaking Basics: Tips & Techniques for Quiltmaking & More.

For quilting supplies:

COTTON PATCH

1025 Brown Ave.
Lafayette, CA 94549
Store: 925-284-1177
Mail order: 925-283-7883

Email: CottonPa@aol.com
Website: www.quiltusa.com

Note: Fabrics shown may not be currently available, as fabric manufacturers keep most fabrics in print for only a short time.